"I always look forward to Father Don's insi
reflections—a Benedictine balance of wit, a
wisdom, human-kindness and compassion, and warm
inclusiveness. Sometimes he challenges, sometimes he offers
comfort, but he never fails to be interesting and engaging. Father
Don's down-to-earth musings shine the light of the Gospel on the
ups and downs of daily living. And now to have them in a handy
collection—couldn't be better!"

> —Canon Robin Protheroe
> Hon. Assistant Priest
> St. Nicholas Church, Brighton, UK

"In these *Musings*, Father Don challenges us, amuses us, and
inspires us, sharing his own acute observations about the joys and
sorrows, the gifts and problems, of being human. He writes out of a
long life lived by the Rule of Saint Benedict and uses his many years
as a teacher and his deep working knowledge of the Psalms, the
Gospel, and the wealth of the whole Christian tradition to help
deepen our sense of what it means to be a Christian and a Catholic
in today's challenging world. It's a very useful book, not one to
whip through in a single sitting but to read slowly and carefully—
a good-natured companion for us on our individual human
journeys. It's also a delightful read."

> —Carolyn J. Dewald
> Professor Emeritus of Classical Studies
> Bard College

"Bits of wisdom from a life well-lived, expressed with elegant
simplicity."

> —John A. Muse
> Presbyterian Church USA

"In such a wise and gentle manner, Father Don provides relevant and motivating messages in *Musings*. Rooted in Benedictine tradition and the realities of life, his words are a spiritual compass that provide the gift of introspective and focused reflection."

—Susan Lynch Vento
CSB/SJU Alumna, Class of '76

"Father Don's writings span the spectrum of human experience and emotion—love and faith and happiness, loss and longing and disappointment . . . [his] reflections come with wisdom that sometimes supersedes those experiences, enabling him to connect with readers on subjects that he has never personally lived."

—Dave DeLand
Executive Director
Saint John's University Marketing and Communication

"Join this captivating Benedictine monk on his fascinating journey through life. He speaks to every one of us, giving us an understanding of matters concerning our faith. His insightfulness is truly miraculous."

—Tom Baldwin
Attorney
Dublin, Ireland

Musings

A Benedictine on Christian Life

Don Talafous, OSB

Oct 1, 2019
Lena — Blessings
on your life and
work —
Don Talafous OSB

LITURGICAL PRESS

Collegeville, Minnesota

www.litpress.org

Excerpts from the English translation of *The Roman Missal* © 2010, International Commission on English in the Liturgy Corporation. All rights reserved.

1   2   3   4   5   6   7   8   9

Library of Congress Cataloging-in-Publication Data

Names: Talafous, Don, 1926– author.
Title: Musings : a Benedictine on Christian life / Don Talafous.
Other titles: Meditations. Selections
Description: Collegeville : Liturgical Press, 2019. | Summary: "A collection of reflections offering hope and encouragement in the face of the sadness and suffering of our world selected from the author's "Daily Reflections with Fr. Don Talafous" posts written for the blog Pray Tell"—Provided by publisher.
Identifiers: LCCN 2019015982 (print) | LCCN 2019981290 (ebook) | ISBN 9780814684726 (pbk.) | ISBN 9780814684979 (ebook)
Subjects: LCSH: Christian life—Catholic authors—Meditations.
Classification: LCC BX2350.3 .T345 2019 (print) | LCC BX2350.3 (ebook) | DDC 248.4/82—dc23
LC record available at https://lccn.loc.gov/2019015982
LC ebook record available at https://lccn.loc.gov/2019981290

To Adam Herbst

Preface

I muse on what your hand has wrought,
and to you I stretch out my hands.

Psalm 143:5-6

I present these brief reflections as hopeful and encouraging for the reader in the face of the sadness and suffering of our world. Most gratifying among the responses I get to the reflections on the internet is that they are (1) inspiring; they help the reader face life with hope, even joy. And (2), I'm consistently told, "They make me think." While these reflections come from the mind, heart, and computer of a Catholic Benedictine, readers further tell me they speak to many people, Christian and otherwise, e.g., some of a skeptical bent or minimal relation to organized religion, many from a variety of religious backgrounds, and believers of differing degrees of fervor. The reflections do not quote Benedictine sources regularly but to some degree reflect several decades of life as a Benedictine.

These reflections are not organized according to subject. They appear here as they do in their original internet setting, each day offering a different subject or a different slant on a subject. We've made them identifiable by making bold the first few words of each; in this way readers who would like to find their favorite reflections easily can make their own index on a blank page at the end of the book (e.g., Saint Benedict in his Rule, p. 21).

I must thank Joe Wentzell and Cody Lynch in particular. Joe vigorously promoted the idea of a book, and he and Cody did much of the groundwork for this collection. Their time and work were invaluable. I must thank Brother Richard Oliver, OSB, who, a couple of decades ago, suggested that I put such reflections on the internet. Thanks also to Josie Stang, who has been in effect the archivist for the reflections as well as a helpful critic and "cheerleader." Her organization makes their daily appearance possible. Finally, my colleagues in Alumni Relations at Saint John's University (Collegeville, Minnesota) and the support staff have been generous in support and encouragement. I thank and bless them.

Pivotal suggestions or admonitions made to me over the decades may be thought-provoking for you. Most of them were made once only and with some impact.

The first of them, however, was made often, going back to my childhood. It came from my mother. My behavior brought it out of her enough times that you hope it had some lasting effect. By way of reproach she repeated a saying seemingly of Irish provenance: "Smile and the whole world smiles with you; cry and you cry alone." As she used it on me, pout or complain could be substituted for cry.

The second shows some continuity with the first. A confrère in seminary with me, who was several years younger, in some exasperation threw this at me one day: "Quit the complaining." It touched a nerve and, no matter how poorly I may have followed the injunction, it has remained an ideal.

The athletic director at this university gave me this next one shortly after I became university chaplain. Though I had been ordained about four years, I was still terrified of public speaking. After one Sunday Mass where I had preached, he caught me and said: "Slow down; we can't understand you." I was attacking my fear of public speaking by rushing the homily to get it over with! After that I began to record my homilies as I practiced them and made a great effort to slow down.

As chaplain in the pre-electronic age, I published a weekly newsletter. A revered English professor told me: "Shorter items get more attention; people are put off by long paragraphs and don't read them." This I have been very conscious of and, I hope, is to your benefit.

The optimism and hope of Vatican II's documents expressed a
view of what the church should be. For example, "The church . . .
is held, as a matter of faith, to be unfailingly holy"; the church is
"the spotless spouse of the spotless lamb."[1] It would be a brave or
out-of-touch commentator who would push those terms in today's
media climate. Some disenchanted hearers would laugh; others
might say, Are you kidding? Victims of clerical abuse would not
be able to forget the trauma and lasting pain. Laypeople, victims
of sexual abuse or not, likely are asking themselves: Should I stay
in the church? Why stay a Catholic? At least one article, by Drew
Magary, states a harsh negative: "The Catholic Church Doesn't
Deserve Your Forgiveness" and the text includes lines like this:
"The Catholic Church deserved to run out of second chances a
long time ago."[2]

Some must ask themselves: Why stay with such a corrupt and un-
trustworthy organization? Many thoughtful Catholics have probably pondered that. Others of us, hearing of the suffering and
anguish of victims of sexual abuse in the Catholic Church, think
also of its effect on the young. One group at the church meeting
(Synod on Youth, October 2018) puts it this way: "A Church that
cannot be trusted is simply incapable of reaching out to young
people in an effective way."

Cardinal Cupich (of Chicago) picks up a "good" in all this: "The
pain such publicity causes the church 'is a small price to pay if it
liberates people [the abused] who came forward.'"

Can troubled Catholics separate belief in the church as the body
of Christ from the institution pictured daily in our media? Can
we find, see, meet Christ in the same place where all this abuse
has happened? What reasons are there to stay with it? Can the
church still point to Jesus Christ, its true center and reason for
existence? Each of us may need to think and pray about this. Those
of us who see some or much good in the church need to ponder
these issues, discuss them, and pray about them. Finally, Cupich

says: "Beneath that anger is also a sadness in the hearts of many people that they know we can do better."[3]

Our working years are often spent managing, taking charge. But eventually there comes a time to "let go." Preparing for this or even thinking of it is often difficult enough. Happily, life itself has been training us for "letting go." We move from the breast to bottle, from basketball to bingo. Time, circumstances, and growth involve letting go of a position, letting go of nights out with the boys or the gals. Some of this has been smooth, natural-seeming; other elements only happen "kicking and screaming." Forty-five-year-old Brett says one of the toughest was getting rid of those slacks with the 34-inch waist that had been hanging in the closet for years. Any one of us with a little reflection can think of many times when we've had to let go of some practice or position. Politicians pondering whether to run for reelection after thirty years in the same office get the publicity, but you and I face similar decisions.

With age and experience there comes the inevitable need to leave some work, some position, some happy, even cushy spot. Letting go of our control and direction, of our enterprise, our position, our children, our mobility, our independence. The words of Jesus to Peter toward the end of John's Gospel (21:18)—no matter the context—seem an apt description of the human trajectory: "When you were younger, you used to fasten your own belt and to go wherever you wished. But when you grow old, you will stretch out your hands, and someone else will fasten a belt around you and take you where you do not wish to go."[4]

Letting go of our driver's license likely sums up the trials and terrors of letting go for many of us. No matter our age, perhaps *now* is the appropriate time to do some thinking and praying about taking up, taking on—*and* leaving behind and letting go.

The scene is semi-rural central Minnesota. Ruth, a clerical worker at the local university, is driving the ten miles from home to her work with her college-age daughter sitting beside her. She comes upon a young black man, no hat or gloves on this cold 15-degree morning, standing on the side of the road trying to flag down some help. Near him is a car with the flashers on.

Ruth stops and finds out that the young man has been delivering the local newspaper to residences; his motor has died; his cell phone is not charged. Several cars have passed him unwilling to stop and he has gone to a number of homes where he has just recently delivered newspapers, but no one answers the door. He explains all this once Ruth has taken him into the warm car and as he enters, he says, "You must be good Christians." Ruth admits that she and her daughter are Christians, descendants of German Catholic immigrants who populated the area in the mid-nineteenth century. Like her recent forebears, she comes from a large farm family of eleven children.

Once in the car, the young man called EJ, Nigerian by birth, phones his Ohio-born wife, the mother of their three children. It will take her about a half-hour to meet him. Ruth must get her daughter to the college by 8 a.m. and all three drive there. Then, she takes EJ back to the site of his dead car and they wait a few minutes for his wife to arrive. Recounting it, Ruth says, "I didn't think of anything but that somebody in trouble was standing out in the cold. They must've thanked me about thirty times." In the office, coworkers hearing Ruth's story admiringly congratulate her.

Commencement: Unless one knows the graduating senior, questions and answers can be tricky. What do you say? "What will you be doing after graduation?" "What happens next?" "Where will you be?" "Do you have a job?" "Are you going to college/graduate school?" "Have you had any job interviews?" "Do you have any job offers?" "Were you accepted at that engineering school?" Depending on the person and your relationship, these can be embarrassing or a happy opportunity to tell you some wonderful news.

Answers may or may not come easily. "I'm going for my master's/ PhD at the university." "I've had three job offers; not sure which one to take." "I got that job at Target." "I've had several offers, but I'm waiting for a better fit." "I'm excited; I've been accepted at Saint Benedict's." "I'm waiting to hear from the Peace Corps." "No idea right now." "I'll be living at home for now." "I've been accepted to med school." "I'm going to law school after a year volunteering." "I've got applications in at a number of companies." "I'm waiting to hear from a graduate program in biomedical studies." "Oh, I'll find something."

Those of us who have found our niche might be thankful we don't have to go through that search again. Or, we simply marvel at such an open future. Too, we may be in a position to provide the graduates with the "experience" they need. Let's pray that the young have and keep high hopes and face a future full of welcome surprises. For the graduates and for all of us—some words from Francis, Bishop of Rome: "Look to the past with gratitude." "Live the present with passion." "Embrace the future with hope."[5] (Others say similar things but quoting Francis reminds us of the hope and joy he disseminates.)

One of my sunnier reflections prompted a demur or challenge from a reader of another faith tradition. The reflection he referred to dealt with fear and the Christian's response of confidence and trust in the Lord. In part the writer, Ron, wrote: "On trusting God—while I appreciate the sentiment, it is still coming from someone whose material existence is secure, who lives in a lovely place and has no worry of not having a place to sleep, clothes to wear, food to eat, access to toilets and showers—with no threat of violence. This is not true for 99 percent of the world." Possibly this is the only one of these reflections that Ron had ever come across. I say this because I think that these reflections *do* face war, crime, poverty, oppression, racism, etc. Most readers, I gather from the feedback I get, expect some hope and encouragement from these couple paragraphs in the face of the truly tortured world around us. Reflections in which I gave illustrations of civility on the streets of San Francisco have been welcomed by readers who find it reassuring to hear of such humanity in an urban area.

One very fundamental premise of these reflections is the Christian's faith or trust in Jesus Christ whom we believe has surmounted death and evil not only in himself by resurrection but for all who put their hope in him. Ron closes by identifying himself as a follower of a faith tradition that does not give Jesus Christ this central position. Other faith traditions in their own way face the problem of evil and the concomitant one for us earthlings of despair and discouragement. I think that believing in Jesus Christ does "make all the difference."

Meeting Erich and Andy, twins returning to college late in August, I correctly guessed it was their senior year. "Yup," Andy said as Erich chimed in, "Where has the time gone!" Clearly more astonished than questioning. Somewhat insensitively, I added: "And it only accelerates!" Precious, precious time! So cherished in retrospect and so slippery in the present. What can we do? Time only seems to stop when we're (1) bored and/or wasting it or (2) forgetting time and maybe space in some wonderful moment. Hearing a young person say that he or she is bored or that something is boring plunges a knife in the heart of many an older person. "Yesterday when I was young / So many happy songs were waiting to be sung."[6] Older people are even more conscious of how the years run away. Being bored, of course, at times is the result of an economic situation that doesn't allow escape from a numbing or stultifying situation. Some of the blame goes on our economic system. At other times it is at least partially our fault; there is much we can do about it. Curiosity, for example, is not simply for two-year-olds. A little imagination can suggest something we can inquire about, do, should do: turning our attention to someone less fortunate, volunteering, simply getting out of ourselves.

To be brutally realistic, of course, most of us have wasted or will at some time waste time. Edith Piaf may not have had any regrets but we may. Someone (in *Maryknoll* magazine) has put it almost tearfully: "Oh would that I had but an extra day or even hour to set things right or make up for so much wasted time. I'd live each precious moment to the full and share with all this miracle called life."

The marriage ritual sees the love of bride and groom as a reflection of God's love for us. We hear less, however, about extending that to all human love. But isn't all love (in less demonstrative cultures, "friendship") the way God's love for us is made flesh, something we can experience? Catholic life presumes that God's grace—God's love—ordinarily comes to us through earthly signs or material elements. If oil, water, words, gestures, bread and wine make God's love present to us, then the touch, the words, the loving presence of another person belong there too; for instance, other friends besides the spouse. To expect everything from a spouse or any one person would be a crushing burden; we need to recognize God's love in other friends.

We need the love or friendship, apart from gender or sexuality, that makes us say things like "How did I ever deserve this?" or "My whole life is changed because Mary loves me" or "Just thinking of Hank fills me with joy and gratitude." An Italian might say, "A day without Ben is like a dinner without wine."

For most of us, God's love needs to be seen or felt. Certain types of spirituality try to contradict this, saying things like this: You should not be concerned about whether anyone loves you.—If you love God, you don't need human love.—Expecting human love is egotism. No, love is as necessary as food. And there are degrees in human love. We may have many people kindly disposed toward us, willing to help us, but very few with whom we can share our thoughts, desires, and griefs. Such persons are bound to be a rarity. More casual friends stay on the surface. Given all that, God's love comes to us through some earthly means, and what is a more powerful assurance of that love than the bliss or joy we have when another's love is clearly shown or a human voice says "I love you"?

Here is a practice any of us might think about for Lent (and beyond) that does a lot of good for others and demands something of ourselves. Susan writes: "This is a Lenten idea I enjoyed that got away from me. A woman, now ninety-three, used to have me to dinner quite frequently; she has been in a nursing home now for some years. I started writing her once a week twelve years ago." (We're talking here about a letter, sent in a stamped envelope to a street address, maybe even handwritten! Typed, of course, is better than nothing.) Similarly, she began writing to some nuns who shared her interest in making greeting cards. "I sent each a box at Easter with candy, rubber stamps, and card-making supplies. One was ninety-eight and had never gotten a package before. It made her cry. So I sent the package yearly and wrote once a week."

The particular practice might suggest any number of variations in frequency or to whom. For example, to some homebound friend, family member, or neglected old man or woman, a prisoner, a service person in the Middle East, a disabled person, someone who did us a great favor once upon a time, a parent(!), etc., etc. Or a call, an email, a text message. Or a visit with some regularity, a card, a letter, a gift. With a little imagination, we could all think of something similar that would mean so much to someone or brighten his or her life, surprise them. A phone call to a friend from years ago or far away. Chapter 25 of the Gospel of Matthew will suggest some other possibilities.

Early in this new semester an admissions counselor introduced me to a new student and his mother, both from Sweden. The student bowed deeply from the waist. (I doubt that this is going to catch on among our first-year students.) The student and his mother were not your stereotypical blue-eyed, blond Nordics, nor was their name Nordic. The counselor explained that the family had emigrated to Sweden from Iran a couple of decades ago. If the "Father" part of the introduction triggered the bow, it was more likely of Iranian origin than Swedish. Subsequent elegant manners on the part of the student added to my impression that I was witnessing another example of multiculturalism on our campus.

Vard is one instance of a much more diverse student body than twenty, even ten years ago. Current students have the advantage of sharing dorms, classes, activities, and social life with students of Muslim, Buddhist, Hindu backgrounds, from Communist countries, students of color, students from inner-city Los Angeles and Dallas, students themselves immigrants or of immigrant parentage (of course, in a way, that's been true for several centuries), etc. The student directory now includes beside names like Peterson, O'Brien, Kowalski, Winthrop, Schmidt, Onofrio, and Coulumbe, new names to master such as Cheung, Cortez, Duong, Fujita, Gao, Jayasooriya, Zhang, and Kimeu. If we, students and staff of the university, are open, this new reality can build bridges and decrease racism, intolerance, and discrimination. Francis (aka the Pope) told the young people in Kraków on the 2016 World Youth Day, "We adults need you to teach us how to live in diversity, in dialogue, to experience multiculturalism not as a threat but an opportunity. Have the courage to teach us that it is easier to build bridges than walls! You will be our accusers if we choose the life of walls, of enmity, of war."

In his book *Road to Daybreak*,[7] Henri Nouwen writes of preachers and writers on religious matters: "Occasionally the main fruit of speaking (or writing) is the conversion of the speaker!" Occasionally? Well, maybe the conversion itself is not always effective. But *normally*, I think, the preacher *is* preaching to himself as well as to his hearers or readers. Otherwise, how would he or she know "our" weaknesses, etc.? A few centuries ago Luther made the same point and many writers, preachers, realize that what they are saying to an audience inevitably is also aimed at their own reformation. "We" and "us," therefore, are more appropriate in such material than "you." "You" is appropriate for Jesus, not for me.

If, for instance, the readers of these reflections thought that the writer had perfectly realized the ideals and way of following Christ that he writes about, they would be pretty disappointed by meeting and observing the writer! When he urges the readers to be positive, generous, joyful, and full of trust because of the resurrection, when he sets patience with a fourteen-year-old as an ideal (the writer may not have teenagers but there are other targets!), when he discusses boredom at religious services, he probably knows what he's talking about; in any of these he's trying to prod himself. As "you" pray, hope, trust, and try to be loving and non-judgmental, as you pray for patience and gentleness in your daily dealings with others, pray that this writer does the same, acts with patience and gentleness, is full of trust, free of judging, sympathetic, alert, and focused at worship, etc. Include him in your prayers.

"I was born and grew up in Asia and was taken to a non-Christian service by a nanny. My parents never went to church, not even once, but after returning to the US, made me go to church by myself." That helped kill any interest the writer might've had in religion. At eighty, he has no part in organized religion or faith. But he says: "Your daily messages help me a lot even though I am not sure what I can believe in." He does agree, for instance, that religion should be *a way through* life, *not an escape* from it. Many of these messages resonate with him, he says, but the ones on faith "not so much." Lacking faith, he aims to "be nice, do meaningful work, and have the courage to face each new day as I age." A retired professor touches on related issues. She writes that her beloved daughter is somewhere between atheist and agnostic. This is "one of my biggest sorrows/regrets . . . My own sense of God's love and support are so important to me that I grieve that she does not have this consolation." On the other hand, this daughter is "a lawyer for the indigent, a public defender (on the West Coast). My belief is that she meets God every day in his broken, human children." Many of us must have a similar experience with immediate family or close friends who don't share our faith but fulfill the words of Jesus in Matthew 25. (Google it!)

Wise and eloquent David Brooks wrote of similar issues in *The New York Times* when he mused about how seemingly rudderless young people deal with grief, pain, disappointment, or sadness. Avoiding explicit mention of religion, he says they are best prepared when there is "a fervent commitment to some cause, some ideal or some relationship." He quotes Friedrich Nietzsche: "'He who has a why to live for can bear almost any how.'" People can endure and do much if they are "idealistic for some cause, . . . tender for some other person, . . . committed to some worldview that puts today's temporary pain in the context of a larger hope."[8] Much to pray about and think about!

At a local coffee shop in San Francisco's North Beach at 8 a.m. one sees the "regulars." They greet each other with well-worn words:

> Good morning. / How are you? / What ya' doing? / Well, the rain has stopped and the sun is out. / Hi, Vince. / Where yuh been? / We missed you yesterday.

Such "small talk" seems nearly universal. Of course, it differs from culture to culture, gender to gender, even neighborhood to neighborhood, etc. Among some and in different venues this may all be more demonstrative, accompanied by a whoop and a big hug. On a college campus I'm familiar with, the most frequent bit of such small talk is a slurred "howzigoin?" No detailed answer expected. Small talk in itself is not full of content or significant material about North Korea or even the local BB team. It's simply friendly. The words are a verbal equivalent of or an accompaniment to a touch, a pat on the back, a handshake, an arm around the shoulder. They are reassuring, friendly, without being heavily weighted. With them we reassure people in our little part of the world that despite the horrors of our world, there remain some solid and comforting things like friends, acquaintances, good neighbors, and even love.

No matter what preoccupations—money, business, worries, the stock market, that teenager—small talk points to our basic, decent, and non-threatening solidarity with others. There are, of course, those who simply plunge into: "About that Olson contract." Or, "I think George was completely off track." A friend tells of jumping right away into serious matters and being brought down to earth after a few minutes of heavy stuff by the friend saying, "Good morning."

Some words are charged with feeling, vibes, associations: lone, lonely, loneliness, alone, lonesome. One or the other is the engine behind many a song or poem. For example, "None but the lonely heart / Can know my sadness / Alone and parted / Far from joy and gladness" (Goethe/Tchaikovsky).[9] Or, "I'm so lonesome I could cry" (Hank Williams Sr.).[10] After saying that God has taken away friend and neighbor, the last verse of Psalm 88 shocks with: "My one companion is darkness." A Peace Corps volunteer deposited among villagers speaking a unique dialect says, "I was so lonely I cried myself to sleep for days." These few examples barely touch the depth of pain these words can evoke. Many of us have experienced this almost indescribable pain. It could be the sadness of "empty nester" parents; the longing ache for love mixed with sexual desire of an adolescent; the heartbreak of a broken relationship; the disorientation and shock of the widowed; the isolation of an older person bereft of peers and forgotten in a nursing home; the dazed and unsure feeling of a new student away from home.

Is there some meaning in this for the life of a Christian? Is it like physical pain, illness, sin, betrayal, disappointment where at least in retrospect we can find something resembling purpose? Is it a setback in our life or a step toward something better? How does loneliness relate to our life in Christ? Is it our equivalent of the cry of Jesus from the cross: "My God, why have you forsaken me?"

Let's end this foray into the subject with a little hope and light. (More on this subject another time.) Can we, presuming we are not ourselves in the throes of loneliness, can we do or be something for others caught in this misery? (*Sensitivity and caution required!*) "I was lonely, emotionally crushed, etc. You came to my help? You comforted me? You befriended me? You consoled me? You joined me in the cafeteria? You . . . ?"

"Wow, what an experience!" Or, "I wouldn't want to go through that again!" When we use the term *experience of personal events,* we usually refer to something difficult or tragic like the death of someone close to us, our daughter's cancer, or the narrow escape we had in a car accident. Or we refer to some delightful and memorable event in our life like the completion of grad school, the birth of a first child, or a particularly satisfying evening with a friend. But in between these highs and lows are the more humdrum and routine times that may predominate. The days and weeks that go by so uneventfully. To stick with less than satisfying work or daily visits with the love of our life when, because of dementia, she no longer recognizes us takes a less newsworthy kind of courage.

It has been said that the real test of any good action or virtue, the real proof that we have some good habit, is *perseverance* in it. Even spending a week or two in a poverty-stricken venue repairing houses, while clearly a good thing, is not the same as living one's life in a decaying neighborhood. It's the staying with something when it's boring, even painful at times, that deserves the medal. The commonplace, the humdrum, the tedious, the repetitive, the useful but irritating action, these are the unsung aspects of human life. The work of farmers and vine growers, the patience day in and day out of day-care persons, of nurses, of office workers, of a spouse coping with the chronic illness of her partner, or of parents dealing with the cancer of a two-year-old or with the ups and downs of an adolescent, etc.—don't these point to a generous heart, which is not material for an exciting film or the evening news? As we look back at this soon-to-be-over year, faithfulness might be a good lens through which to review it. Ignoring our culture's criterion of success, Mother Teresa put it this way: "God has *not* called me to be *successful*; God has called me to be *faithful*."

Some years ago, after arriving in the Bahamas for a two-year stint, I was so pleasantly surprised by what turned out to be a regular sight. Almost daily, you saw the local bishop, Leonard Hagarty, OSB, dressed in clerical suit, riding his motorcycle (as did all of us Benedictines). But there was always this: his face lit up by a wide, genuinely happy smile, one of his hands almost always off a handle (!) waving to someone on the street, somehow dodging potholes, chickens, and other challenges. In a letter written by him to the people of the Bahamas, he spoke about how much more effective preaching or teaching was when it was accompanied by witnessing. People listen best to preachers and teachers, he said, when their lives match their words. Further, he said that he always felt very strongly that you witness best to the good news of the Gospel when it really *sounds* like good news. On his motorcycle, radiant as he kept waving greetings, he made it really *look like* good news too.

Bishop Hagarty's *words and bearing* are echoed in Pope Francis who says Christians should not "have a funeral face" because "pessimism" is not for Christians.[11] A severe critic of Christian faith, Friedrich Nietzsche, made the same point from his stance. I para-

phrase his words: Christians would have to sing with more conviction to persuade me to faith in their redeemer and they'd have to
show that faith in happier faces. Our faces should be those of re-
deemed people, of those who know the joy that comes from the
forgiveness of our sins, a closeness to God, and trust in God.

Being grateful is one thing. It is an especially rich and gracious
attitude toward life, a way of living. But what moves gratitude out
of ourselves to make a positive impact on others is our expression
of that gratitude in some way. A former student of the university
who graduated in 1973 with a major in chemistry models such
expression. Retired after some thirty-plus years as a physician, he
wrote to his professor of analytical chemistry whom he credits for
his happiness in the medical profession. (This was a letter sent via
the US Post Office, pen on paper, in an envelope with a stamp!)

Jeff's message to the professor, also retired, was this: "Dr. RF, I
don't feel I have ever had a chance to fully express my gratitude to
you for your encouragement when I was applying for medical
school. I was grappling with doubts and uncertainty. You strongly
encouraged me to continue with my medical school applications.
You instilled in me a sense of self-confidence. In my mind, I can
still picture meeting with you in your office and can still feel the
sense of gratitude that I felt after our meeting. I cannot possibly
expect you to remember me, but I do want you to know how posi-
tively you affected my life at that point." At the end of his letter to
Dr. RF, which he copied to me, Jeff wrote: "I read some time ago,
that if the only prayer we ever say is 'Thank you' and if we truly
mean it, then we are right up there with the saints."

So often in many of us, a sense of gratitude may well up at times,
but to get to the point of actually thanking individuals who have
done or meant so much to us is where we falter. We put it off till

it finally becomes material for the eulogy. Besides, of course, family members whom we so easily take for granted and owe so much, there are individuals such as the one cited above. In his thank-you note, Dr. RF said what a pleasant surprise it was. I imagine there are many such people—teachers, coaches, mentors, counselors, advisors—who would be happily surprised by such a letter.

(The repetition of this topic among these reflections is partly due to the need of the writer to express it, and atone for his failures.)

Elsewhere I may have mentioned my theory, now my conviction, that the age of two is the peak in the human trajectory. Sure, I used to think it was around twenty-six or twenty-seven but I've changed my mind. The enthusiasm, curiosity, and energy of a two-year-old are never matched again! It's to be hoped that we are often able to muster enthusiasm as life goes on. We may keep or develop a probing and ever-questioning mind. But, even granted that, the *energy* will certainly diminish. My adulation of two-year-olds got a boost recently upon hearing on public radio that the favorite music of a particular two-year-old was Beethoven's "Ode to Joy" from his Ninth Symphony. (If you don't know it as such, you very likely have heard the melody used for a joyous hymn.) Don't underestimate the little dears! A friend has a four-year-old whose favorite food is Gorgonzola gnocchi! He probably can't pronounce or spell it any more than the other young child can say Beethoven, but it lights up his eyes and whets his appetite!

What more appropriate music for two-year-olds than the "Ode to Joy": they never walk! They always run! They can go, jump, climb, crawl till they finally fall asleep. It's as if they had some conviction about the brevity of human life and are out to soak it up! Do they perhaps think to themselves: "This elasticity and agility, they tell me, won't last. Why waste time just walking—you don't see as much that way. You will never find a table covering to pull off or a lotion to spill if you just stay put! My random movements and undignified waddle will inevitably have to be exchanged for something more sedate, my diaper for a dress or a suit. Laughing might get a bit strained at times. Responsibility and life's setbacks can make it hard to be so carefree and joyful." If you are in the vicinity of a two-year-old or have one or see one, stop and enjoy the joy! And hope that it is contagious! (PS: Especially to you worn-out parents of the little dears: I do know there's a lot of very high, messy, and expensive maintenance involved. Your patience and resilience are my reasons for thinking you deserve canonization—and a bonus too!)

Some readers enjoy my reflections/blogs recounting visits to San Francisco that seem to revolve around coffee shops and Uber drivers! Back in semi-rural Minnesota, one has fewer options. But about five miles from this university is a town of around seven thousand. There one doesn't have to get one's coffee from a gas station since the town is home to a unique coffee shop with its own bakery. An assortment of seven booths, large and small tables, and four or five spots at a bar make for a capacity of around forty or fifty. Throughout the day a steady stream of patrons comes through the door. The clientele? Local card-players seem to meet daily at 10:30 a.m.; people coming from Mass at the church across the street (lots of jay-walking); profs from either of the two local colleges; retired teachers and attorneys; students (not too early however); active or retired businesspeople; members of the two (male and female) Benedictine monasteries.

Many patrons stop in to pick up their latte or Americano and then head out the door; others sit and enjoy coffee, freshly baked pastry, conversation, and greeting familiar faces. Parents have fond memories of good conversations with their college daughter or son over coffee or tea in this user-friendly atmosphere. Lots of small talk and also serious meetings. For example, a retired monk-professor (Ger) stopped briefly at a booth to visit with two college students from China, call her Ying, him Ben. (Incidentally, neither is Christian.) Ben is non-stop exuberant, always smiling, very light-hearted, verging on a laugh. He was trying to build a closer relationship with somewhat reluctant Ying. The three sat and had some light conversation. After Ger left, Ying said to Ben: "Well, if Father Ger thinks you're a good man, then I'll be your girlfriend." Happy Ben says: "What happened? We were talking about math and all of a sudden she's willing to be my girlfriend!"

For those enjoying a coffee on site, their drink can be served in locally made pottery. Greeting cards, also by a local artist, are available from a rack; their originality and wit can hold their own with San Franciscan counterparts. Daily soups, sandwiches, and specials are written on a large blackboard. San Francisco coffee shops will have their regulars but there's always room for anonymity; in this setting, anonymity is hard to come by. They say that it's pretty difficult to get noticed in San Francisco; in this coffee shop you're bound to be noticed and greeted by a buddy, an acquaintance, or a friendly stranger.

The college chaplain remembers how fearful and uncertain he felt while talking with a student at a time when the expansive work of Vatican II had not yet germinated. A student named Bob had come into the college chaplain's office. Attending Mass on Sundays, he said, left him so unmoved and bored that he couldn't "stand it." The possibilities for variety introduced after Vatican II had not yet become a reality. To make matters worse, the Mass at the time was still in Latin. After more discussion, the chaplain finally said to

Bob: "Well, Bob, why don't you skip it for a month or so and see if that helps?" Trained in a moral theology that had little time for conscience, the chaplain thought to himself: "What have I done? Did I go too far? What right did I have to cancel the 'Sunday obligation'?" The teaching and rules of the church were presented in such a way that *they were your conscience*; you didn't have to worry about any personal decisions (God forbid!).

How refreshing it has been to hear Pope Francis: "We [pope, bishops, priests] have been called *to form consciences, not to replace them*."[12] By thinking that everything is black and white (that is, by *telling people* what their conscience is), he says, we discourage people who are doing their best as Christians but cannot at the present reach the ideal in every situation. (They are in the gray area.) Most of us, you and I, know in conscience that we should love all our fellow humans, but some of them (including me, for example) make that pretty tough to do.

Under several previous popes, we have had examples of bishops claiming to decide for laypeople what their conscience is on particular issues. But most Catholic Christians have recovered some trust in their own conscience. Francis supports this when he says that conscience is the most "secret core" and "sanctuary" of a person. There each one is "alone with God."[13] To the annoyance of some Christian churches, this exercise of conscience has often led to walking away from the church. Almut Furchert has put it this way: "Søren Kierkegaard used to say: you first have to reflect yourself *out* of Christianity in order to come back to it anew."[14] Possibly this leads to more convinced and committed Christians, people who experience trust in Jesus Christ and his loving embrace as the heart of belief, of faith.

Psalm 119 is the longest Psalm in Scripture. It is made usable for public prayer by dividing it into some twenty-two sections. Verse 67 (among others) suggests some fruitful reflection on a very basic subject: "Before I was afflicted I strayed, but now I keep your word." Another translation reads: "I used to wander off until you disciplined me; but now I closely follow your word." We hate to think of this, that the only way to a fuller life in Christ is through affliction or something else which "disciplines" us. It's that same lack of relish with which we look forward to any cross. We resist seeing any good in a real and present affliction—for instance, an illness, chronic pain, an emotional torment, a severe loss—and so, of course, fear it.

Sometimes the pain is softened for us: it creeps up under some other guise and before we realize it, we are already being "improved." At other times, our trouble may accompany something else that we really desire and enjoy—pleasing work, good company, etc. It's a bit like a parent giving a small child some unpleasant oral remedy by disguising it with some sweet. Events seen as so contrary at the time become the unexpected door to a happy and fruitful life we might never have imagined otherwise. One door closes, another opens, goes an old saying. Adversity and even misery are often good teachers. In baptism the pattern of our Lord's suffering, death, and resurrection becomes ours also. "Before I was afflicted I strayed, but now I keep your word." Loving God, may your strengthening grace be with us, in us, no matter what pleasant or unpleasant happenings may come!

Saint Benedict in his Rule is no exception to the frightening (to some, disgusting) conviction that spiritual growth requires that the serious Christian regard herself or himself as "poor and worthless" and "that a man not only admits with his tongue but is also convinced in his heart that he is inferior to all and of less value" (Chapter 7: Humility).[15] Personal experience tells me that such a conviction can only come with a great deal of self-knowledge and the latter only with a great number of years! Rightly, I think, loving and thoughtful adults don't crush the exuberance and spirits of the young by telling them they are worthless. (How would you phrase that on a résumé!) Another side of the issue is the advice St. Francis de Sales writes to a young correspondent: "While we must have patience with others, we must also have it with ourselves." In fact, if we are really serious about developing our love of God, he says we need to be *more patient with ourselves* than with others!

When and if we get to the point of seeing ourselves as "inferior to all," it will not be a depressing squelching of all self-worth. It will be a liberation from stress and straining, freedom to surrender ourselves fully to trust in God's love, forgiveness, and initiative. We are not masters of the universe—or even masters of everything in our little lives. We can relax: finally, it's up to God. Further on in the same letter, St. Francis de Sales says: "Our imperfections are going to accompany us to the grave."[16] The goal of Christian life is not to sculpt some interior equivalent of a Greek god but to embrace the truth in the words of the hymn that God "calls and claims us as His friends / And loves us as we are."[17]

As we begin any Lent, many of us could do better than "I will give up my daily beer/desserts/watching *How I Met Your Mother*/etc." How about enlivening my life in Christ with some daily and personal—that is, *unique to me*—prayer? Public prayers, like those in the Mass, become mechanical and remain formal unless they have the daily accompaniment of personal, private prayer. More often than not, it's you or me who is standoffish in our relation with

Jesus. He demonstrated real neighborliness by taking on our flesh and life and even more than "his" share of suffering. The Lord Jesus is easily available in the Eucharist, in Scripture, in our fellow human beings, and in all of nature. Everything else we might think of for Lent is, I think, fairly petty compared to developing a genuinely personal prayer life. (If yours is blazing ahead and well advanced, find something else to read!)

If Lent is about restoring and renewing my relationship with God, that can only be done using some of *my* language, with some daily communication about *my* needs, *my* hopes, *my* worries, *my* failures. The kind of communication—and even silence—that exists between friends. No one else is going to renew *my* baptismal promises at Easter. The prayers of the Mass are for a gathering of individuals, purposely applicable to *everyone present*, while being *unique to no one*. They are somewhat like our "How do you do?" "How are things going?" or "Good morning." Only a prayer like that of writer Anne Lamott, "Lord, help me not to be such a jerk," can come from my unique self-knowledge and experience. With such frankness and familiarity, we're on the way to genuine and liberating trust in the Lord.

Elsewhere in these reflections I have made a point about how ideal it is if, in our prayers of petition, instead of spelling out for God what God must do, we are able simply to trust God's loving care for us. More reflection on my experience and that of others tells me to modify that. My remarks about simply trusting God still, I think, describe the ideal situation, are still something we should aim for. But . . .

When we're in any difficulty or pain, large or small, any terror, fear, great concern for others, worry about others or ourselves, etc., we will almost automatically pray for specific help. It can go all the way from praying as we watch a wrestling match or a hockey game that "our" team win to praying that our spouse overcomes that cancerous tumor. We pray that the estranged couple are able to save their marriage; we pray as we fall from our bike that we don't break anything; we pray that the pesky stomach ailment go away; we pray that Dad's dementia does not get any worse; we pray for successful treatment of the neighboring four-year-old's leukemia. Very likely, no matter how deep our trust in God's loving intentions in our regard, we still let the immediate need come to the fore.

Psalm 147 says that God not only calls each star by name but "heals the brokenhearted" (v. 3). God stands at the origin and support of the universe and at the same time listens to our sorrows and worries. Though some of our requests of God may seem pretty petty, who are we to put limits to God's magnanimity or willingness to heal? Prayer is its own reward. Just the fact of praying is basic to any genuine Christian life. It changes us—now or later. How it works, what it does, etc. Ultimately, trust in God's love will out!

Francis, Bishop of Rome: Over fifty years ago, John XXIII spoke of opening the windows to let some fresh air into the church; they were opened a bit but then someone must've felt a draft. The Bishop of Rome elected in 2013, Francis, seems interested not only in opening the windows but the doors also. "Catholic" after all means universal, all-embracing. In a now famous interview, Francis said: "This church with which we should be thinking is the home of all, not a small chapel that can hold only a small group of selected people." Various adjectives have been used to describe Francis's approach, but one that I really prefer is "down-to-earth."

Not only is there room for many people, many types of people, in the words of Francis there is also room for mystery in regard to the church's teachings, a recognition that every bit of teaching is not on the same level of importance or certainty. For example, he said: "The church sometimes has locked itself up in small things, in small-minded rules. The most important thing is the first proclamation: Jesus Christ has saved you." Echoing Vatican II, he underlines: "The dogmatic and moral teachings of the church are not all equivalent. The church's pastoral ministry cannot be obsessed with the transmission of a disjointed multitude of doctrines to be imposed insistently." He says that otherwise we risk "losing the freshness and fragrance of the Gospel."[18]

"Fresh air and fragrance": no matter what time of the year, it feels like spring!

Several decades ago I was struck by hearing an elderly Benedictine, certainly no radical, say that *he regularly asked the prayers of his deceased mother.* Many of us are too hung-up on the process of canonization by which the Catholic Church formally declares someone a saint, a person of outstanding holiness. I think most of us live surrounded by saints! (What follows is heavy on parents and spouses, but there are many other categories.) Jesus put the requirements plainly: love God and love your neighbor. What about those parents who forego world travel to enable their college-age sons and daughters to study abroad? They stay at home and on the job— and together—while their offspring enjoy privileges they never were able to afford. Apart from parenthood, how many of us get up several times a night to take care of a sick child and then get up at 5:30 a.m. and drive to the office? And once there, we are expected to be alert, pleasant, energetic, prepared, even imaginative!

Laypeople don't have organized groups like the Benedictines, Jesuits, Salesians, any religious group in the Church to push the process of "canonization." The Home and School Association is unlikely to do it for John and Kay. Often canonization seems more like a Hall of Fame for high-profile persons in the Church. And to require "miracles"? (One could, by the way, argue that, biblically speaking, miracles are not empirical matters to be verified by science and witnesses.) Aren't there miracles in the perseverance and patience of such men and women—hospital and hospice workers, caregivers, social workers? In the sacrifice of time and comfort they make for others, often not simply for a paycheck but with love beyond the job description? Aren't there miracles in faithfulness, compassion, forgiveness, generosity, hope, joy, loving care, perseverance, patience, gentleness, etc.? I feel that I am telling you the obvious. . . . Let's celebrate and be grateful for these neighbors, family members, and friends!

Note on a restaurant menu: "Cell phones in use will be confiscated and turned into stew."

Most of us learned with a little maturity and experience that doctors, clergy, teachers, public officials—that none of these should be immune from questioning. That, even though often idols of our childhood, they do have faults. But do we question technology, in practice an idol in our society?

So often it seems that if technology shows that something can be done, we take that as the final word. Much of what technology presents to us is driven at least in part by the desire of the manufacturer or inventor to make a living—or a bit more! In the last decades (it has been that fast!) we have been presented with gadget after gadget which, as one claim goes, makes it possible for us to take everything in our life with us in this little rectangular item. Do we ask ourselves whether that's something we should do?

All this is often presented as an increase in communication. Communication? Yes, but *apparently with anyone but the people we are with at the moment.*

We know and we see people walking around wired, oblivious to those who are with them or whom they meet or pass. Anything, anyone, but the present, the here and now. How about turning the machine off to be present to the people we're with or who are in our presence?

That note on the restaurant menu was very apt: "Cell phones in use will be confiscated and turned into stew." The idea is that, for one thing, we should appreciate the food before us and, it is hoped, even more, value and enjoy the people we are with. Why come with Ted and Jill to dine and then spend our time talking to Bill or Angie in Shanghai, Madrid, or North Dakota?

And, further, what about enjoying some silence in our lives? Do our ears and minds have to be filled with talk or noise all the time? Rabbi Abraham Heschel writes that silence and prayer leave an opening for God to speak to us.

The writer and illustrator Maurice Sendak (*Where the Wild Things Are*) was interviewed a year before his death in 2012. At the time, he was in his early eighties. He spoke with emotion and candor about the sadness of seeing friends die before him; he said, "I cry a lot." In passing he said he had no belief in an afterlife, but a moment later said he still hoped to see his brother again. He went on: "I am in love with the world. . . . There are so many beautiful things in the world which I will have to leave." He ended with: "Live your life, live your life, live your life."[19]

We believe that death sends us back into the hands of the loving God who brought us into being in the first place. Still, that faith and trust compete with "love for the world." And, too, there is a struggle to make that trust *felt* more, more visceral than simply cerebral. As with Sendak, we feel there are so many beautiful things that we will have to leave . . . My list: friends, music, theater, reading, the changing seasons, dinner with friends, cheese, wine, chocolate, laughter and humor, beauty in people, big cities *and* solitude, travel, espresso coffee, languages, people-watching, sunrises and poetry, two-year-olds . . .

At my age, surely not far from death, I try to act on the belief that the best preparation is generous, loving use of the present, of time and of opportunities. With Sendak: "Live your life." Live the present wholeheartedly. With appreciation for all that is, all I enjoy . . . Visiting people in hospitals—for instance, the sixty-four-year-old woman who simultaneously has liver and heart problems, diabetes, breathing difficulties, an infection in the leg—I realize how quickly my life could change. Live life, live it now with generosity, hope, gentleness, and joy.

In the words of a pre-Metallica song: "There will never be another you." The implication is that the genome of each of us is unique. To say, however, that any one of us is *irreplaceable* would be a stickier matter. Unique seems unquestionable. However, irreplaceable is more accurately used about what we do and how we function than about who we are. Nobody else will ever be this Ang Kim, this Mary Smith, or this Isidore Melankowski. But others will be that middle school English teacher, that Wall Street trader, that worker in concrete, that engineer, that pope, or that coach.

Whatever else it might be, the resignation of Pope Benedict XVI or, where the writer lives, that of a very successful eighty-five-year-old football coach of fifty years, can be seen as recognition that "I am not irreplaceable." Someone else will become Bishop of Rome and someone else will coach football. (The coach, by the way, does not take credit for giving the pope an example.) At the same college another in his mid-eighties (let's call him Ben) is still employed in alumni work. Ben tells his immediate boss that he, Ben, hopes he will have the grace and perception to resign when he becomes unable to fulfill his position with any energy or imagination. Possibly this is something many of us need to think about even at a much younger age in regard to our position. Am I a burden or an obstacle? Do I need to change? Do the people I work with and for, do they need a change?

An element in all of this must be a more interior matter—our estimation of self, our view of "irreplaceability," and our humility. A phrase going back to Pope Gregory the Great says the pope should regard himself as "servant of the servants of the Lord." Being at the service of others finds a lot of support in the teaching ("I am among you as one who serves"; Luke 22:27), and even more in the life, of Jesus Christ.

At any moment, thanks to technology, we seem submerged, if not overwhelmed, in and by human suffering. There is always some catastrophe with unimaginable sorrow and suffering; there are famines and drought, so many human conflicts all over the world, present to all of us no matter where we are; there is what seems to be an epidemic of cancer, crime, oppression, injustice, etc. A couple centuries ago, thanks to slower and limited communication, people would only hear of so much suffering elsewhere belatedly and piecemeal, if at all. Today there is no escape from it. We are inundated, like it or not. Trusted religious leaders anguish over it, trying to get a human handle on it. Attempted explanations and understanding are, for all our effort, simply inadequate. They may tell us how tsunamis and earthquakes and war happen, but we're all left with "Why?" or, often, "Why me?"—whether in our hearts or in cries and screams. Philosophers and theologians, when thinking about it, call it a problem; better, call it a mystery.

The issue requires at least these two responses: (1) In the midst of universal horror and pain, it may be best to emphasize once again, and realize our solidarity with, all suffering human beings—whenever and wherever—and draw what consequences we can. We are one human race; we share one planet. (2) We can and must pray. As with disease or catastrophe, we attempt to explain fumblingly how prayer works. But what will help in actuality is simply to pray, best of all with trust in prayer (based, we hope, on personal experience), and trust in the God who in so many ways has shown us love and will show us love.

"Oh LORD, You will not leave my soul among the dead, nor let your beloved know decay. You will show me the path of life, the fullness of joy in your presence" (Ps 16). This is typical of the psalms we highlight during the Easter season, full of lines that refer to the resurrection of Christ and our own. Hebrews tells us that Jesus was crowned with glory and honor after tasting death for everyone. By his death he "free[d] those who through fear of death had been subject to slavery all their life" (2:14, 15). A note in the New American Bible tells us that the fear of death is "based on the false conception that death marks the end of a person's relations with God." Our very existence is due to God's love (mediated through our parents) and death returns us to that love, to the God who loves us. We live in that hope, Henri Nouwen writes, and "when we face death with hope, we can live life with generosity."

We share daily in the suffering, death, and resurrection of Jesus in the many falls, disappointments, hurts, and tragedies of life and in the ways these are surmounted. For example, whenever we ditch our selfishness to be generous and loving; when a healing touch or word overcomes illness and discouragement; when forgiveness allows us to go beyond bitterness and self-pity; when faith promises what the misfortunes of this life cannot give. In renewing our baptismal promises yearly at Easter, we once again commit ourselves to sharing in the life and death of Jesus, trusting that sin is overcome by love, suffering by joy, hatred by forgiveness, death by life. "Oh LORD, I cried to you for help. Oh LORD, you have raised my soul from the dead, restored me to life from those who sink into the grave. . . . So my soul sings psalms to you unceasingly. Oh LORD my God, I will thank you forever" (Ps 30). Alleluia!

Benedict in his Rule says that guests should be received as Christ. In his day, part of this was washing their feet after walking on dusty roads. Welcoming every guest as Christ seems a pretty steep ideal when we are faced with grumpy or demanding guests. Incidentally, receiving guests *as Christ* often disarms some more forbidding visitors! Hospitality is an easily available, down-to-earth way to honor Christ. Having said that, we may still need encouragement regarding the "how" of receiving guests today.

Hospitality has to mean much more than carrying out the mechanics. Most of us in our experience of the "service industry" have noticed how practitioners vary. An indifferent maître d' or sour server has already lessened our enjoyment of a dinner. And, of course, we have to allow for the fact that people doing such services have their bad days, their personal sorrows and pains to deal with. (But, do any of us, no matter what our work, have to share all that with others?) Just to give a guest a key, point them toward a room, even carry a bag—all that is lacking in luster if we are indifferent or surly. Offering a smile or some warmth in our greeting doesn't seem excessive. Most of us have learned how to smile at a very young age. If that still seems beyond our capacities, at least our words can be welcoming: "Good morning, how are things?" "Hello, how may I help you?" "I hope you're enjoying this beautiful day." "Let me know if you need something."

Of course, we patrons are also part of it. St. Benedict speaks of the importunity of visitors; they may come at inconvenient times or be taxing. In the course of writing this, I illustrated some of this. A busy server in a restaurant failed to bring my order as I had asked for it and I was a little testy. Fortunately, as I sat eating I recalled what I had been writing and with at least a smidgeon of humility apologized.

To my mind, two situations are equally mesmerizing: watching the ocean waves rolling onto the beach, the glint of the late afternoon sun on the waves of a lake or, on the other hand, watching the parade of human beings in a large city. Some say that the drive of evolution is toward ever-increasing diversity. Sitting in a coffee shop on Montgomery Street (San Francisco) weekdays between 8 and 9 a.m., one easily believes it (apart from all those North Face jackets).

Bankers, street people, businesspeople, service people, truck drivers, students, and tourists pass by endlessly varied in size, gait, color, dress. The short and the tall; the Mediterranean, the African, the Nordic, the Asian; hurried or sauntering; paunchy or petite; blonde and brunette, bald and bushy, bearded (that's in, especially for men), gray and going, curly or shaved; bedraggled and bejeweled; smiling or somber, worried or confident, resolute or tentative; tottering elders or twerps. Serious or silly, grim or glad; in flip-flops or stilettos, stylish or just-out-of-bed, stiff or casual, drab or dandy;

eager or dragging, hobbling or hearty, wired or gawking, striding or stumbling; helmet or baseball cap, rotund or pencil thin; deposited and kissed on the cheek by the driver, tourists with children, couples walking hand-in-hand, tots clinging to Mom or Dad.

And all of this is only exterior, external, only what one can see! Think of the variety within: worries, hopes, desires, ambitions, plans, anxieties, preoccupations, love and hate, joy and sorrow, disappointment, satisfaction or anguish, anger or gratitude.

The Bishop of Rome received generally very favorable reaction to an interview given in August 2013. One line resonates with many: "I see the church as a *field hospital* after battle."[20] A recognition that we all have been wounded or at least show signs of wear from "the slings and arrows" of life. We need healing, a project for both Word and Sacrament, for the touch of the Lord who loves us. Ordinarily that love comes to us through another human being's compassion and sympathetic understanding. An often-used prayer entitled "Hail, Holy Queen" has a line about "poor, banished children of Eve." With little children this has often come across as "poor, *bandaged* children of Eve," an unwitting intuition of this truth! That certainly fits with "field hospital."

We are all engaged in either healing or wounding by how we interact with our fellow human beings, with those we live with or work with, with those we simply encounter occasionally. It seems that developing a sensitivity to whether we are healing or wounding others takes time and experience, experience of successes and failures in our relations with others. Increased sensitivity and understanding of what it means to love our neighbor may require time and certainly requires prayer.

Yogi Berra put it succinctly and accurately: "Wherever you go, there you are." While change, a vacation, "going to the lake" as we say in Minnesota, a day off, getting out into the country—or into the city, a movie, dinner out—while any of these can give us temporary surcease or a lift, it may be a bit like a diabetic taking some sweets to avoid a crash. The problem in our life may be more profound.

The ancient Roman letter-writer Seneca answered a friend's complaining letter thus: "Are you surprised, that after such long travel and so many changes of scene you have not been able to shake off the gloom and heaviness of your mind? You need a *change of soul* rather than a change of climate. . . . Do you ask why such flight does not help you? It is because you flee *along with yourself*."[21]

While we work to allow God's grace to form us more after the image of Christ, we'll need patience with our present self. Some self-acceptance may be required so that we can get on with our life. Surrendering ourselves to God's grace, trusting that we have been taken up into the strength of the Lord, these with time can make this self less burdensome as we experience little changes for the better. In many ways all life is patient waiting and receptivity.

An image from my first years as a priest in a lower Bronx parish remains vivid. I had been called to a tenement; ambulance personnel were preparing an elderly lady, all alone in the apartment, for transport to a hospital. She was distraught, teary, and frightened. Adding to her distress was the fact that the ambulance people were tying her with cloths to a straight-backed wooden chair, a necessity because of limitations in the building. I was probably more shocked than compassionate. My seminary education had been more about orthodoxy and law than compassion and if I'd had any human sensitivity, I would have accompanied her.

Though it may not seem so brutal, the lot of many elderly is similar: often bereft of family and friends of their age, casualties of economics, torn from the familiar and cherished, placed among strangers, no matter how caring, in a care facility. Eventually the obituary will read: "The family would like to thank the staff of South Memorial Hospice for their compassionate care." Very likely this will be true. Take Alicia, for example, who had fallen several times in her home. Alicia is one of these. In her upper eighties now, she is faced with trying to make new friends or watching more TV in one week than she'd watched the previous fifty years. After a failed attempt to invite another resident to the snack room for coffee, Alicia is discouraged. How many such overtures to strangers can you make at eighty-eight? The psalmist was there: "Friend and neighbor you have taken away. My one companion is darkness" (Ps 88:19).

Is this old man or woman someone's parent? She or he can feel not only uprooted but abandoned. What a huge difference a handwritten letter to open and re-read, a visit, a surprise, a phone call, the gift of a favorite snack or drink would make. Or to have some familiar person come and sit for a while, maybe read to them, reminisce, or say a prayer. Or bring some photos of grandkids. A wordless touch, a smile may be all that's needed. "I was in a nursing home and you visited me."

"**Give me again the joy** of your help. With a spirit of fervor sustain me" (Ps 51). That verse might be good to pull out when one feels less than excited about the upcoming day, work, or other matters.

Or, when feeling especially lacking in fervor. We can, of course, do simply natural, human things that enliven or galvanize. Repeating the phrase above as a sort of mantra might help to change the attitude or mood.

"Give me again the joy of your help." Help me, Lord, to be grateful for my life and work and to show it by my spirit, by some joy. How you or I pray, of course, may not suit everyone. Despite an occasional bad or less-than-fervent mood, we may be able to recall some happy elements within, e.g., a generally very happy life, good work to do, and wonderful people to work with. A little reflection may bring up thoughts of my good fortune relative to many others; urge me to show some goodwill and love to all those around me. We could end up thinking there is really no serious reason for not feeling grateful and even joyous.

"With a spirit of fervor sustain me." As is typical of Hebrew poetry of biblical times, the parallel sentence or phrase often repeats the previous one with some slight nuance. The joy of your help is practically identical with the spirit of fervor. And if all this doesn't help or work, maybe I have the option of staying out of the way of other people or taking a walk.

The funeral of a decorated (Purple Heart) World War II veteran once again illustrated the many ways in which parents influence their offspring. The four sons and two daughters, as they greeted so affably those in attendance, brought back vividly the graciousness and ever-generous smile of their deceased father. Dad probably didn't have the kids practice graciousness but, like the gait and language we pick up from parents, these were such a part of this man and his wife that the children simply breathed it in. What patterns parents, teachers, coaches, mentors leave with children and young people!

A character in Barbara Kingsolver's short story "Quality Time" clarifies matters for an expectant mother who is concerned about "what to pass on" to her child. Parenting, the responder explains, is "3% conscious effort and 97% automatic pilot." She illustrates: "It doesn't matter what you think you're going to tell them (children). What matters is that they're right there watching you every minute, while you let the lady with two items go ahead of you in line or when you lay on the horn and swear at the guy that cuts you off in traffic."[22]

All in all, what we say or how we consciously try to act, these are a poor second to the kind of person we open ourselves to becoming by grace, prayer, the example of others, and a good conscience. The good person in Christian thought is not in the first place the result of analysis and plotting out one's actions but a *consequence* of turning oneself to God and others in praise, self-forgetfulness, love, and service.

"In your house I am a passing guest, a pilgrim, like all my ancestors" (Ps 39:13).

For Americans, *pilgrim* could as well be immigrant or migrant. People proud of their ancestry in America were descended from immigrants (unless they were Native Americans). But in the middle nineteenth century in the United States, a political party was formed called the "American Party"; popularly its members were known as "Know-Nothings." The members were mostly descendants of earlier immigrants from places like England and Scotland. They were appalled at the prospect of the country being flooded by Irish Catholic immigrants fleeing famine and destitution. Cartoons depicted a boatload of Irish Catholics arriving with a fully vested pope at the helm about to tread on American soil. Businesses with employment opportunities posted signs in their windows: "No Irish need apply." Events went further. Riots on the East Coast resulted in the Know-Nothings burning two Catholic churches, a Catholic school, and a couple of convents. At least twenty people were killed in riots.

German Chancellor Angela Merkel and her country have been notable for a more welcoming stance toward migrants fleeing poverty and war. She says: "I am pleased that Germany has become a country with whom people outside Germany associate with hopes. . . . That is something very valuable when one looks back at our history" (a reference to the Nazi period).

"In your house I am a passing guest, a pilgrim, like all my ancestors."

Psalm 92: "It is good to give thanks to the Lord, to make music to your name, O most high." Psalm 25: "To you, O Lord, I lift up my soul." Psalm 145: "I will extol you, my God and King, and bless your name for ever and ever. I will bless you day after day . . . The Lord is great and highly to be praised; his greatness cannot be measured." Those not familiar with the psalms still hear or sing such psalm verses, at least in Mass. They usually are like the opening verses quoted here: words of praise to God, exclamations about God's greatness, and thanksgiving. Usually nothing about Bill's cancer, that mass shooting, or war in the Middle East. Some might say: "nothing practical." Many must think: "Why bother? God doesn't need praises; they're just a waste of good time and energy." But *we* need them!

Most of us have gone through a phase in our younger life when we were repeatedly asked after receiving a gift: "Now what do you say?" Learning the answer was meant to teach us gratitude. Similarly, thanksgiving for our existence, for this universe, for our life, for friends, for the life, death, and resurrection of Jesus—thanksgiving for all this most frequently must be learned. Left to ourselves we take everything—life, parents' love and care, friends—for granted. Some reflection should tell us that they are anything but to be presumed. All is a gift, a gift from the Creator. Gratitude is only the appropriate response. Psalm 30: "And so my soul sings psalms to you unceasingly. O Lord, my God, I will thank you forever."

In the course of an otherwise routine surgery, Diana's husband, Mike, suffered a number of strokes. Recovery and return home took nearly three months. At his side or in the hospital all this time was Diana, from the beginning on December 10 till February 28, the first day she did not see Mike during this period. Understandably, her first reactions, as written in the CaringBridge journal, were: "I was so angry and felt God was picking on us . . ." But not for very long: "I decided we weren't being picked on at all, but rather chosen." This refrain continued through Mike's paralysis and coma to mobility, crabbiness even, and joking, ups and downs. Long before the end of this journey, she was able to write: "*God is good.* We have been taken down a path that is not of our choosing, but one that brings new opportunities each day. So many people tell me how they are praying and I know he is listening to them all. Mike has so many people that love and care for him, as do I and our family. *Life is so good.*"

"O, wonder! / How many goodly creatures are there here! / How beauteous mankind is! O brave new world, / That has such people in't!" (Miranda in Shakespeare's play *The Tempest*).[23]

As Mike prepared to return home, Diana wrote: "I have learned so much . . . I realized how much God is with us—he is simply a prayer away. I am changed by this and from what I hear, others are as well. Some are praying for the first time in years." The italics above express *my* amazed awe. It doesn't take anything as serious as paralysis to unsettle my peace and trust! Diana gives me much to ponder. And you?

The Rule of Benedict reads in chapter 53: "All guests who present themselves are to be welcomed as Christ, for he himself will say: I was a stranger and you welcomed me. . . . Proper honor must be shown to all" (53.1-2). The Rule echoes Matthew 25 where Jesus says that what will count in the final judgment is whether or not we took care of the sick, clothed the naked, visited those in prison, etc., *and welcomed strangers*. In so acting, Jesus says we are doing it to and for him. In those turbulent times, the guests were not necessarily Christians. Benedict specifies a bit further: "Great care and concern are to be shown in receiving poor people and pilgrims, because in them more particularly Christ is received; our very awe of the rich guarantees them special respect" (53.15).

Pope Francis spoke to the American Congress of those who present themselves today at the doors of the world's wealthier countries: "Migrants are our brothers and sisters in search of a better life, far away from poverty, hunger, exploitation and the unjust distribution of the planet's resources which are meant to be equitably shared by all."[24] His talk brought some legislators to tears, but not to any welcoming action. A country often termed the richest in the world has been slamming the doors to migrants and immigrants at the behest of fear-mongering politicians. On the twenty-fifth anniversary of the fall of the Berlin Wall, Pope Francis warned that there are still too many walls: "Wherever there is a wall, there is a closed heart. We need bridges, not walls!"[25]

The United States once understood itself as a refuge with no distinction of religion, race, or place of origin for immigrants. A bronze plaque on exhibit at the Statue of Liberty (words by Emma

Lazarus), calling America "Mother of Exiles," reminds Americans of their nobler ideals. In part, the poem reads: "Give me your tired, your poor, / Your huddled masses yearning to breathe free, / The wretched refuse of your teeming shore. / Send these, the homeless, tempest-tost to me, / I lift my lamp beside the golden door!"

Jim, in his mid-fifties, suffers from terminal cancer and is receiving chemo. A friend from the same Communist-ruled country, a convert to Catholic Christianity, suggests that he pray. Jim says: "I do not believe in that." An atheistic background could explain that or the dying person might object to prayer if we regard it as magic—zap, you get what you ask for, simple as that. In Luke's Gospel (11:5-13), after a story urging persistence in prayer, the literal words of Jesus come close to that: "ask and you will receive; seek and you will find; knock and the door will be opened to you. For everyone who asks, receives . . . ," etc. An explanation is needed.

Even without long-term experience of prayer, when making a request in prayer, we have to allow God freedom to respond as God will and to realize that we are not equipped to dictate the response. Only enough regular practice of prayer will convince us of this. We can, of course, pray for a specific outcome but why not make that conditional? God may have other outcomes "in mind." The words of Jesus quoted above point to that in extravagant language: *Steadfast prayer is effective. Only by persistent effort and regular practice do we come to know what prayer can do.* It's not magic; it is often something much more life-changing and effective in the long run, which escapes our limited vision and imagination. The great Danish Lutheran Søren Kierkegaard said it best: "Prayer does not change God, but changes the one who prays." Knowing our differences and our so-varied circumstances, change in any one of us can mean many differing outcomes and be extremely varied in scope. For example, a change in our attitude toward what we were praying for; more trust in God; more gentleness with others; more acceptance of our life; less whining; more love within a family; more gratitude.

Who's "coming"? Whose "advent" is it? Jesus Christ, of course, Lord, Son of God and Son of Mary. *Most immediately* he's coming across the Mediterranean, the Rio Grande, through the Balkans, driven from his home by war, poverty, persecution, or oppression. In Matthew 25, Jesus tells us that it is him we are serving when we help the stranger, the hungry, the thirsty, the naked, the imprisoned, and the sick. Today, these are migrants and immigrants from Syria, Africa, Asia, Central and South America. He is present in these as well as in the congregation at Mass or in the tabernacle.

Yet, as Pope Francis has pointed out, there is an "epidemic of animosity" against people of other races or religions that hurts the weakest in society. And "how quickly those among us with the status of a stranger, an immigrant or a refugee become a threat, take on the status of an enemy . . . An enemy because they come from a distant country or have different customs. An enemy because of the color of their skin, their language or their social class. An enemy because they think differently or even have a different faith."[26] We of the "first world" are stewards, *not absolute owners*, of most of the world's wealth and goods. We act as if we had an unquestionable right to them, that we can build walls and fences to "protect *our* property and goods," to hug them to ourselves rather than share some of that with our displaced and suffering brothers and sisters in this *one human race*. Most of us North Americans are the sons and daughters, the descendants, of immigrants from Ireland, Germany, Russia, Italy, Eastern Europe, Scandinavia, etc. They came as those strangers Jesus speaks of with the hope of the better life most of us now enjoy. A welcome to today's strangers and displaced is a welcome to Jesus.

In the time immediately after Pentecost, one hears frequently at Mass this particular prayer: Lord, send out your Spirit, and renew the face of the earth. Or, Come, Holy Spirit, fill the hearts of your faithful and kindle in them the fire of your love. In the same spirit, ever-hopeful Pope Francis urges us to be open "to the God of surprises." Never say "this is the way it has always been done." That self-defeating attitude so often implies that we can't expect anything new to come from our trust in God.

Say we pray and *continue* to pray, especially *for* something, and there is no immediate and specific response to our prayer. Aren't we in this way saying that we are open to surprises, to an unexpected answer to our prayer? For instance, we pray for a family member who has advanced leukemia. Despite persistent prayer, the leukemia is never cured. But, as a result, the whole family has developed a heretofore lacking relation to the living God. Another unforeseen result might be to fire up the comatose faith of the doctor. These would qualify as surprising outcomes. There are, of course, others. But let's leave other surprising responses that would never occur to us up to God's "ingenuity." Even if our prayer is not prayer of petition, but persistence in some form of meditation—some simple quiet receptivity to God—that, too, carries with it a trust in the love of God and in God's surprising effects in our lives.

Francis goes on to say: "The Spirit is the gift of God, of this God, our Father who always surprises us. The God of surprises . . . Why? Because he is a living God, who dwells in us, a God who moves our hearts, a God who is in the Church and walks with us and in this journey surprises us. It is he who has the creativity to create the world, the creativity to create new things every day. He is the God who surprises."[27]

At a campus football game I was four times mistaken for Father Waldo and once for Father Hobart. The next day a cyclist pedaling by as I walked called out "Father Kirk." For a moment, with a slight knowledge of Buddhism, I thought: perhaps I've reached the state of "no-self." A little reflection, however, assured me that I was far from anything so noble. It doesn't take much reflection to realize how well acquainted I am with selfishness, self-centeredness, and self-seeking. How remote St. Benedict's ideal remains: "No one is to pursue what he judges better for himself, but instead, what he judges better for someone else" (Rule of Benedict, The Good Zeal of Monks, 72.7).

Not too long after the Father Kirk episode, I got into a car only to find pasted to the dashboard an oh-so-timely word of Jesus, Matthew 16:25: "For those who want to save their life will lose it, and those who lose their life for my sake will find it." This is a steep word of Jesus about how we open ourselves to transformation into his likeness. The death and resurrection of the Lord and our sharing in it is the model of this profound and unsettling ideal: Jesus truly gave, surrendered, earthly life on the cross out of love only to receive new life in the resurrection. We shouldn't think of this only in terms of our death. It's present in those moments when we give ourselves to others in some demanding service; when we recover from sin, despair, some tragedy; when we forget our own interests to further those of others; when we put aside our time, schedule, and priorities to serve something larger than ourselves. (Doesn't this sound like what parents do daily?) Very likely the opportunity to lose our self in order to find it is available to all of us in many of life's demanding situations. The Word of Scripture and Sacrament make the Lord present to us in his self-giving so that our self becomes more one with Christ, becomes more our true self.

Encountering so many old friends at the reception/lunch after a funeral, one might feel some guilt for having so much fun at such a serious time. Typical of this fun is the experience of the writer. Barely inside the church for a funeral he was happily surprised to run into Valerie, a former student of his, now a Lutheran pastor. In this part of the world most of us are used to renewing bonds at such times. True, if the funeral were of a young person whose death leaves parents and friends overwhelmed with sorrow, laughter and camaraderie will seem questionable. If the deceased had been suffering for years, family and friends will likely see death as a relief. In such a case they will be accepting and comfortable with reminiscing and laughing about old times, seeing old friends. A priest serving in alumni relations at a Catholic college says that the shorthand description of what he does is: "Fun, food, and funerals."

In many ways, these very happy times when we meet old friends after a funeral at a lunch or reception are expected and welcomed. Rediscovering old friends while losing another is the way it has to be. We renew friendships with people who have been a part of our life. We meet them changed as they may be by illness, life's "hard knocks," successes and disappointments, tragedy and love. And, to touch on the "food" part of the line quoted above, as with so many important moments in our lives, our getting together happens *in the context of a meal*. Once again we are happily reminded of the uniquely *human* element in eating. We are not merely renewing our physical stamina. We are celebrating friendship and our solidarity in the human community (as we do in the Eucharist) over ham sandwiches, Jell-O, coleslaw, and chocolate chip cookies—or the equivalent—and a lot of laughter.

Revelation in popular media means that such and such a politician or celebrity is spilling all about his or her now-off relationship or a senator is reporting the latest from the Better Lighting Committee. In other words, new disclosures. At times some have thought about Christian revelation in the same way. That is, we think revelation occurs when God gives us teaching (truths, dogmas) about, for instance, the commandments, marriage, authority in the church, biblical truth. If understood this way it's easy to see how a pope or bishop, as has happened, could spend time declaring a theologian's writing on one of these matters to be erroneous. For example, he or she "is no longer a Catholic theologian" or "not to be employed in a Catholic university."

But revelation in Scripture is more about *God's disclosing God's self to us*, not in statements but in the words and actions of God's Son Jesus Christ. In Jesus we see that God is loving, forgiving, even self-sacrificing. In other words, a person we can relate to once we reflect on his life, a person who can draw us into a loving relationship. It's similar to the way we warm up to a new friend, how we discover what attracts us to him or her. Revelation in the Christian context helps us enter a relationship with a person, getting to know and love *the* Person, God. With this understanding, popes and bishops can act like pastors who encourage Christians to follow Jesus, and to know that Christ is in us to make that possible.

From the moment of his election, Pope Francis has emphasized that being a Christian means such a relation with Jesus. And that this brings with it the necessity of caring for Christ's members, the poor, the suffering and marginalized. Working to make others hopeful and happy and our world and environment safe and fair to all. With Francis it is not about hunting heretics or dissidents.

Being a Christian is about an encounter, a loving relationship with God in the person of Jesus and the members of his Body.

The focus of our early decades is on development: physical, intellectual, emotional, religious. Learning to play the tuba, to run the triathlon, to understand tax law or how to do surgery, to grow crops, to care for the disabled, to visit space, etc. Success in our development depends on our motivation, our cooperation, our opportunities, etc. This focus on ourselves (our résumés) continues with advanced degrees, new levels of expertise, promotions, married life, buying a home, etc. We could summarize this part of our life under the term "acquisition or growth," acquiring education and relationships. Part of this earns the term "growing up." Very few dispute the necessity of this. In our life as followers of Jesus, too, there are practices and steps that deepen our relationship to God, e.g., prayer, sacraments, actions done out of love, study of Scripture. And this development in our character almost naturally leads us to think about *what will we do with all this development?*

This growth acquires meaning and purpose when we put it to good use. The second half of human existence justifies all this "preparation" when we begin to give away ourselves and what we have become and acquired. We begin to use our talents, our time, our achievements, our means and acquisitions, our skills, our patience, all our experience and know-how for others, for causes, for the good of our world and our fellow human beings. Volunteering for the homebound and disabled, supporting good causes, spending time with those grandchildren, for instance. Ideally we use what God has given us or, with God's help, what we have acquired or developed for others, for *something beyond ourselves.*

Sitting alone almost anywhere, we have probably heard some acquaintance say: "All alone? No friends?" That may be a good excuse for pointing out the distinction between *alone* and *lonesome*. Of course, they can be the same but by no means necessarily. Alone may indicate a kind of independence or a desire to reflect, pray, think over something, or a weariness from too much "socializing." Further, one can be lonely in the midst of friends, in the midst of many people. When one is truly lonesome ("I'm so lonesome I could cry") or lonely, it usually is for the presence of a particular human being, someone who shares enough with us to assuage that pain. Given how different each one of us is, it's likely that only one or two people can alter the situation. At times it may be possible to have our feeling of loneliness banished by simply being in the company of any mix of human beings.

Our loneliness can be related to the fact that our desire for that just-right intimacy is a desire that no one human can satisfy. Does this ache in our hearts point to God as in that famous line from St. Augustine? Speaking to God he wrote: "Our hearts are restless till they rest in you." Some thinkers, not necessarily believers, speak of a fundamental restlessness that really defines what it is to be human.

Behind the thought of those who equate the physical state of being by oneself with loneliness may be their fear of simply being alone. May not that explain why so many of us have to have a TV or radio going all the time? Are we afraid of being alone? Is silence terrifying? Why are people afraid of silence? What happens if we are silent? Why is silence used as a punishment? What are other uses of silence?

College men's table conversation is often banter, talk about sports or what's going on this weekend. (Or about women.) So it's surprising to join some students at table and have very articulate and unchurched Jake ask me: "Why am I here?" By "here," it's clear that it's not about why he's eating in this place rather than at Joe's Burger. It's more profound.

Having snagged a retired theology prof, Jake expects more. I try my best. "My belief is that existence is a *gift*, not something I asked for or was owed to me. I see my existence as coming from someone or something, for me, God. Understanding it as a gift, I have, not always very faithfully, come to see consequences: I should value every moment and use it out of gratitude in a responsible and generous way. Going further, I see that the end of this existence will take me back to the One whose love brought me here in the first place. And so, at least in my better moments, I strive to live with trust, hope, and generosity."

Though Jake might not answer the same way, he seems to have come to a similar answer. Now in his last year in college, he has been active in good causes and lives responsibly. Following graduation, he will spend a year volunteering his time and abilities at a school in India. Though he might not articulate the answer as I did, doesn't his life demonstrate a recognition that existence is a gift whose meaning we find in how we live it? Francis, the Bishop of Rome, puts the emphasis on *what we do for poor and suffering fellow human beings* more than on *how* we formulate our beliefs.

> *Evening*
> Here dies another day,
> During which I have had eyes, ears, hands
> And the great world round me;
> And with tomorrow begins another.
> Why am I allowed two?
> (G. K. Chesterton)[28]

"In vino veritas" (literally "In wine the truth"); the old proverb reminds us that tongues loosened by alcohol often blurt out truths otherwise kept to ourselves. Another old saying is that children in their naïveté similarly let fall uncomfortable or unacknowledged truths. For instance: an elderly man with a cane was walking out of a funeral home visitation; he finds the exit in the "control" of two young children. A little boy and a girl, presumably his sister, a few heads taller than him, are opening the door. As he goes through the door, the little boy says, "Broken leg." "No," says the man. The little girl offers: "It's something that happens when you're very, very old." There may be other reminders, too, for an octogenarian but this is easier to welcome, coming from such innocence.

The truth about ourselves, about life, can be found, of course, through self-examination or accepting the comments of a friend. But frequently, the genuine truth comes from less likely sources. People who are not our biggest fans can come up with critical remarks or, even in anger, blurt out uncomfortable truths. Even if the source at first raises our hackles more than our self-awareness, there may be a kernel of truth in such remarks. Literature and theater can similarly open our eyes.

It's easy to build up defenses against seeing our true selves and opening ourselves to change. When a season like Lent calls us to conversion, the initial phase may be self-knowledge. Unless we see the issues, it's unlikely we'll welcome the cure. We don't see the Savior unless we see the sin.

A certain strand of Buddhism makes "mindfulness" or attentiveness its essence. Jesus' parable of the sower whose seed falls on various kinds of ground touches the same matter: how open are we to the word of God, the seed? The point of the parable is that God's word can only be effective in us if we receive it well.

Daily experience shows us how difficult it is for us to pay attention to anything. We fall asleep reading the paper, watching TV, in class, during a sermon. Or, if we don't go that far, while the priest is talking about the upcoming Lent or honesty, we are thinking of brunch or wondering where we left the detergent. Why do so many things have to be repeated and in so many different ways? Viewed theoretically it makes no sense; we should be able to hear and take in what is being said to us. Yet how tough it is for us to give our full attention to anything: a parent, a child, our work, a piece of music, even our food. In fact, we often purposely try to do several things at one time to avoid "wasting," as we say, all that time on one thing.

Someone has said that there is no moment so rare as one where we want to be where we are, doing what we are doing. More often our attention is scattered all over creation. We might practice the opposite habit during prayer or at Mass. We could begin by making gentle efforts to give our whole attention to what we are hearing. Instead of fighting in irritation with our distractions, brush them aside and refocus on a word or phrase. Take a word or a phrase like "God is my strength" or "The Lord is with me" and as we sit and find our mind drifting, we just repeat the phrase slowly. And over and over again during the time we're trying to pray. Concentration can grow as a habit.

We are impressed by the love that organizes rescue missions for whole countries or builds chains of children's hospitals in the third world. But we may shortchange the power and value of our own reassuring words, our compliments to the living, our greeting, the time we take for a short, encouraging visit, our interest in another's work, our sympathy in their pain, our coaxing a friend to submit her poems or to run that race. In both instances, we see the power of love to transform and give birth to something new.

But there's more to it. When the Gospel of John speaks of Jesus loving Lazarus (and all of us) so much that he raises Lazarus back to life (John 11:1-45), there is also an underlying condition for all this. Before Lazarus comes out, the stone must be rolled away from his tomb. And so with us, before anyone's love can be so effective in our lives, it helps if we are open to it; the stone must be rolled away. Before a helpful word or bit of attention can do any good, there has to be some receptivity. Even love finds it hard to penetrate a stony heart.

"Got no butler, got no maid, / Still I think I've been overpaid. . . . Got no silver, got no gold, / What I got can't be bought or sold. / I got the sun in the morning and the moon at night" (from *Annie Get Your Gun*).[29] Reminds me of a Zen story of a hermit who while away had been robbed of the little he had in the way of clothes and food. Coming back to his hermitage, he sees the full moon glowing in the sky and regrets not being able to give the robber this beautiful sight. What is most precious to us are often elements that we cannot share with others.

Given each person's amazing uniqueness, it is no surprise that so much cannot be shared or given away. Others often do not understand our interest in some kind of music or movies or theater. They have a hard time seeing what we see in another person. One of the frustrations of human communication is that the way we feel about certain persons or experiences is simply not easily transferable to others. What is most valuable in our lives we often have little choice but to keep to ourselves. The glow we get from these other people and circumstances we almost unwittingly will share with others.

A dear friend, Pat, around sixty-five years of age, writes: "I value your daily message which bolsters my faith especially at times when I find myself apprehensive about what lies in store after our earthly run." Coincidentally, a colleague tells me his six-year-old son Frankie asked: "What happens when people die? What is heaven? What do they do in heaven?" Ten-year-old Ellen chimed in: "Is there purgatory?" To the last, Dad wisely shrugged a "Who knows?" with his shoulders.

Words from St. Paul in First Corinthians (2:9) put it briefly: "Eye has not seen, nor ear heard, nor has it entered into human hearts what God has prepared for those who love him." In a way that says it all. Elsewhere, Scripture dares compare it to the carefree joy and love that characterize a wedding: music, dancing, laughing voices, smiles all around. Or, try this: heaven is the condition where we live in the loving presence of God and of all who preceded us in a way that satisfies all our deepest longings and hopes. Whatever we do in heaven, it's all part of the joy of life with God and with all who love God. Jesus elaborates on the "all who love God" by saying that loving God is "the great and foremost commandment. The second is like it, you shall love your neighbor as yourself" (Matt 22:37-40).

To "love God" seems a pretty airy idea, not something we experience as we do loving a spouse, a parent, children, friends, and many others. Just as we know, even feel, God's love for us through the affection others show us, so don't we normally display our love for God in the love and service we give to other human beings? For instance, loving the person or persons we commit ourselves to, in rearing children, nursing the sick, comforting the suffering, tending the disabled, etc. (See Matt 25.)

"Apprehensive about what lies in store after our earthly run." Probably our greatest fear is the fear of death. Henri Nouwen says that getting past that fear clears our way to live the present generously and freely. We can do that when we look at death as a return "to the One who loves us with a love that was there before we were born and will be there after we die." Once we realize and trust "that we are born from love and will die into love," then evil, illness, and death lose their power over us (*Our Greatest Gift*).[30] Yes, that sounds good but not easy. My best answer to that and my most frequent prayer is: Deepen my trust in your love, dear Jesus.

Even the most devout Christian must have questions at times about how prayer works. How effective is it? Why pray at all? One of the most trustworthy signs of a believer is just the willingness to pray. Our beliefs and our morals are in many ways less convincing signs of our following of Jesus than is our praying. Belief can, at times, be simply a mental thing; the morals we practice are often duplicated by non-believers. But prayer shows a confidence not only that there is a God but that this God is concerned about and able to act in our lives. Prayer makes no sense apart from some trust in God. Though it remains true that none of us may have a sure grip on how prayer works, a belief in it defines us as Christians.

When illness strikes, when someone loses a job, when a marriage is in trouble, when a teenager seems headed for disaster, when an accident worries us, we pray. We trust that in some way, somehow, God will help. Our trust does not mean we have to expect God to change the laws of the universe; it may be something much more subtle. Perhaps as a result of prayer, I or someone for whom I pray learns how to deal with some disaster or cancer. We are probably better off in the long run not trying to figure out what God might or should do and instead trusting that God has ways of which we know so little. Jesus says: "I give you my assurance. Ask and you shall receive, that your joy may be full" (John 16:24).

In the story of Jonathan and David (1 and 2 Samuel), the Bible touches on the topic of friendship. Though celebrated occasionally in the Bible, it doesn't get the prominence we assign to it. But, as so often happens, these famous stories suggest much that is helpful to us, more effectively than some philosophical treatise might do. The backdrop for the friendship of Jonathan and David is their relationship to Jonathan's father, Saul. The latter resents David's popularity and sees him as a rival. To persist in his friendship with Jonathan, David had to put up with his friend's at-times-murderous father. Undoubtedly, each had to be patient with faults in the other, as well as in the relatives. Perhaps that harp with which David soothed Saul got on Jonathan's nerves.

If we are going to preserve and develop a friendship, we inevitably have to put up with less than ideal traits in the other. Not to be willing to do this leads us to a friendless place where we are alone in what we consider our own perfection. Friendship and love require a willingness to persist in affection and intimacy even though every feature of the relationship may not be exactly ideal. Similarly, for sure, the other must forgive inanities or odd, even repellent, habits in us. Friendship is one aspect, one type, of the love Christ teaches. It is worth the effort and the forgiveness it requires of us and these can be sustained by our own relationship with Christ.

Jesus apparently expected that acceptance of his message would bring some joy: "All this I tell you that my joy may be yours and your joy may be complete" (John 15:11). Do we treat joy too easily as a natural quality of some individuals and somberness or even grumpiness as a natural quality of others? Differences of temperament seem pretty obvious, but the words of Jesus suppose that some joy should be a consequence of our belief in the Risen Christ. We can't let ourselves off the hook entirely by pleading a heavy personality. If instead of joy we speak of a positive spirit, an attitude marked by hope and trust, it might be clearer.

For the Christian, some positive and hopeful attitude toward life, based on the resurrection, is not simply another option like whether or not I like bowling or garlic. Belief in the resurrection must have some consequences. We contribute to the world's hope and joy to the degree that it does. And none of us is so independent that how others feel, how they act, what they say, is of no importance to us. Negative, grumpy people in oversupply affect us all. The presence of joy and hope, on the contrary, raises our own spirits. Without being phony, we can still offer the people around us talk and an attitude that builds up and offers hope.

"It is I; do not be afraid!" (Matt 14:27). Along with calming a storm (14:22-36), Jesus with these words confirms for the disciples that he has a special relation to God. "It is I" is a reference to the way Yahweh (God) was identified in the Old Testament. In the context, Jesus is not simply making a theological declaration but reassuring his terrified disciples in the midst of a storm. "I am," he says effectively, "so close to God, so one with God, that you can have trust and not fear."

Yet fear remains a reality of life. And it serves some good purposes: it tells us in a dangerous situation to be careful, act with prudence. The news reports about our cities make many of us fearful and more circumspect; the weather report helps us to be prepared with shovels, flashlights, or adequate fuel. There are plainly many things that arouse fear, both in nature and in our fellow human beings.

But what about fearing God, Christ? Should that be another fear? Reverence for God, awe of God's greatness and power, are understandable and appropriate. But should we be scared of God? How can that fit in with a Christian belief about God? Should we really believe that God delights in keeping us scared? The miracle stories of the New Testament again and again tell us, instead, that we honor God's greatness by trust, confidence. Because God is so great and powerful, we put all our trust in God. Because Jesus is one with God, the Son of God, we expect every good, above all peace and hope, from him.

"Wherever you go I will go, / wherever you lodge I will lodge. / Your people shall be my people / and your God my God" (Ruth 1:16). You probably hear this most often at weddings where couples see in Ruth's declaration to her mother-in-law, Naomi, and her God a good statement of their own commitment to each other. Naomi has lost both husband and sons, leaving her bereft in a foreign land; hearing things are better back in Judah, she decides she must go there. Ruth's words then follow. Ruth's dedication is first of all to Naomi and then to Naomi's God.

Doesn't that reflect the way things usually go? We come to God, we come to understand faithfulness, loyalty, responsibility, commitment, love, first of all through our attachment to some person. In fact, to get back to the wedding, aren't husband and wife supposed to mirror for each other the lasting love and faithfulness of God? Don't most of us learn of these matters through other people, friends, those we love and who love us?

Other people, Ruth's commitment tells us, are so important to us and, vice versa, we are so important to others' faith and hope, whether we realize it or not. It's another way of reminding ourselves that our faith, hope, and love are intrinsically bound up with others. We don't come to God in some disembodied manner but through what we know of relationship from friends. We depend on each other; we influence each other; we support each other—or, on the other hand, discourage or weaken each other. Someone somewhere is dependent on us for encouragement, inspiration, help, whether in word or example. United to Christ we can be other Christs to our world, to each other.

The woman sitting with her back to me in the airport says to her companion: "I ordered a bagel with butter and cheese, and she looked at me as if she had never heard of such a thing." Possibly the snack bar attendant was thinking of cholesterol. Or one thinks of how unique we are, how varied our behavior, how incomprehensible to others our actions are. Travel and varied experience show us continually new, unheard of ways of doing things, customs we could never have imagined, practices that may frighten us a bit, some that undoubtedly offend us. In a village in India we pass a couple, man and woman, conversing as she walks several feet behind him; we ask for a toothpick and are surprised to have our table companion from Tanzania pick one out for us; a friend tells us of the family custom of peanut butter and onion sandwiches; adolescent boys walk hand-in-hand at the Taj Mahal; a woman orders a bagel with butter and cheese . . .

Will travel in the cosmos bring even stranger experiences? Will all our ways of doing things be up for examination? Each broadening of our perspective brings into question much that we have taken for granted. What remains? Do we clutch even more closely the manners and morals of our upbringing and look uncomprehendingly at whatever is different? Does all this perhaps give more meaning to a vision of God as the one sure thing? Or, are we trying to find our anchor in matters that cannot give us that surety, in something other than God who is, as the Psalms tell us, our rock, our fortress, our strength, our savior?

When you think of the tantrums we can throw over an offense or a slight or someone else's mistake, it is easy to see how many a religion has taught that our self-centeredness is the primary wrong in our world. Not only tantrums but terrors of greater magnitude seem so often to originate in me and my importance. Several world religious systems teach that overcoming all sense of self is the key to happiness and salvation. As long as I think of me, myself, mine, I am doomed to unhappiness, lost, says Buddhism. Jesus, of course, teaches that we find true happiness in losing or denying self.

Another way of looking at the obsession with self, selfishness, self-centeredness, whatever we call it, is to see it as an offense against the first commandment, which forbids us having any other God but God. In practice, over-concentration on self can become a form of idolatry: I am all that really matters to me. No wonder a great Irish wit and playwright, Oscar Wilde, could say that taking oneself seriously is really the original sin. One must feel at times that there are two forces in combat in this universe: God and we humans. We resent our creatureliness, the fact that we come from and owe all to Another. Insofar as we let ourselves believe and act as if we were the center of the universe, we're really competing with God. More of a sense of humor about ourselves would be one way to keep us off those pedestals and, literally, down to earth.

We unthinkingly repeat many simplifications and stereotypes about the Bible and Christ's teaching. We talk sometimes as if the God of the Old Testament only wanted fear from us, as if God was some sort of divine terrorist, whereas the God of the New Testament gives and desires love. That is insufficient and exaggerated. We talk as if Peter was set up as a full-fledged pope in the New Testament; just not true. We talk as if the idea of reward and punishment were completely foreign to the God of the New Testament. Or, on the other hand, as if God had a crew of certified accountants keeping track of all we do and adding it up so as to give us the appropriate reward or punishment. Both are too simple.

In the New Testament we hear both that life with God, salvation, is a gift and, on the other hand, that God does reward us. But reward in Jesus' dictionary is not something determined by how impressive God has found us but by how good God is. God rewards us because God is good, loving, generous, not because we have twisted God's arm by our extraordinary virtue. Salvation is God's gift; the good we do is because of God's grace, God's gift in us. Human boasting in the presence of God is completely ruled out. Our relation to God comes down finally to trusting God's goodness, not trying to impress God.

The poet Emily Dickinson wrote that there were two biblical injunctions she had never broken: "Look at the birds of the air" and "Look at the flowers of the field" (see Luke 12:22-31). Possibly if we took them as commands, too, we'd practice more of the carefree trust and confidence our Lord points to in these words. In them, he rebukes our seriousness and worry about work, about getting ahead, acquiring things, position, power. His words address not only the wealthy who wear themselves out getting and safeguarding things but also those with little who can be eaten up with desire for more.

If we could take these words more to heart, they could free us from much that weighs us down. Our desires for position, prestige, power, recognition, influence, our concern not to be underrated, all this would take a back seat to trust in God's care and the value God gives us. Like most poetic words, these are better left to be read and repeated as they are. "Which of you by worrying can add a moment to your life span? Learn a lesson from the wild flowers. If God can clothe in such splendor the grass of the field, will he not provide much more for you, O, weak in faith!"

You shall know them by their love; see how they love one another. These phrases were written in reference to the early Christians; the first to an ideal, the second to a reality, at least in one place or time. As the New Testament insists in any number of places, love should be the defining mark of Christians—love for each other and love for those around us to the extent of working for their good. Until we show that more convincingly and consistently, we may be apologetic even thinking of other virtues. And, in fact, St. Paul says that all the commandments are summed up in this one: love one another.

But, how about a word for hope anyway? In the world of continual disasters, disease, and destruction, that would probably do, next to love, nearly as much for the world. "You can tell a Christian by her hope." And "See how they hope." For Christians, hope means a conviction originating in and sustained by God's grace that evil, disease, sorrow, and sin will not have the last word, that the goodness of God and creation will prevail. And, too, hope is based on love; it's because we know of God's loving intent for our world that we can justify our hope. How to hope? Human effort alone will only produce optimism, which is good as far as it goes. Hope is very much a gift we open ourselves to by reflection on God's word and persistent prayer. Situations that tempt us to discouragement or despair can help us to be more insistent in our prayer for hope.

Asking people who face anywhere from a half-an-hour to an hour or more of commuting in bumper-to-bumper traffic only to arrive at a very trying job, asking them to add something in the way of penance during Lent seems callous or the rumination of someone living in an unreal world. I'm tempted to think that such suggestions about adding some penance during Lent were thought up by people living lives devoid of the ordinary stresses involved in making a living. Their placid lives may have needed the seasoning of some humanly devised and artificial struggle.

In any case, most of us, it seems to me, should not look upon Lent as a time for some unusual practice but for either patience with what we must do or a more generous fulfillment of what family, work, and world already require of us. In other words, brightening up, tightening up, cleaning up, improving the way we do what God requires of us.

So often Bard, a retired professor at the college, meets former students visiting campus. Those in their forties, fifties, and sixties may show signs of aging: graying hair or no hair, perhaps a paunch, a less jaunty gait, etc. Almost replacing a greeting will be some comment to Bard like: "You haven't changed a bit!" or "You look the same as you did thirty years ago!" Very often Bard will respond: "You mean I haven't changed in thirty years? There has been no improvement? That's discouraging!"

Bard has served as chaplain and taught theology. So he teasingly takes the comment about not having changed to refer to a stalemate in his interior life! In other words, his faults and limitations are still there or have grown worse. But the church, with her annual pre-Easter season of Lent, aims to help us become more profoundly like Christ, to renew once again our birth in Christ at Easter. Our interior "physiognomy," in other words, should be, not more lined or sagging, but more radiant and youthful, full of hope and trust. And consequently more joyful, free, and at peace; transformed, remade in the image of our Lord Jesus Christ. St. Paul writes: "Now the Lord is the Spirit, and where the Spirit of the Lord is, there is freedom. And all of us, with unveiled faces, seeing the glory of the Lord as though reflected in a mirror, are being transformed into the same image from one degree of glory to another; for this comes from the Lord, the Spirit" (2 Cor 3:17-18 and earlier in chapter 3). "To those who welcome the Spirit, the Spirit gives each day a fresh liberty and renewed joy and trust" (Cardinal Suenens).[31]

Coventry Patmore, a nineteenth-century English poet, in a poem ("The Toys") refers to having slapped his little son: "Having my law the seventh time disobeyed, / I struck him, and dismissed / with hard words and unkissed, / his mother, who was patient, being dead." Later sorry and penitent, the poet stops by the boy's bed, sees his lashes still wet from sobbing and that he has arranged some toys by his bed. Touched, Patmore prays to God that when we lie dying God will remember "of what toys we made our joys" and will say of us, "I will be sorry for their childishness."[32] In other words: I'll forgive, take into consideration the toys and distractions, not all so innocent, that so often have taken up their time.

Patmore echoes some comforting lines in Psalm 130: "If you, O Lord, should mark our guilt, Lord, who would survive? But with you there is forgiveness" (vv. 3-4). We may judge each other harshly at times but because "our ways are not God's ways," we can trust God who knows us more profoundly to be more lenient. "To know

all is to forgive all," as has been said, may put it too extremely, but
. . . Certainly, there are some tougher words about sin. But Psalm
130 deserves to be kept in mind. Appropriately we often use this
psalm at funerals: "If you, O Lord, should mark our guilt, Lord,
who would survive?"

At the risk of sounding very much out of touch, living in another
age, etc., I'd like to urge that we learn to relish doing one thing at
a time. Why out of touch? Well, it's certainly fashionable and makes
one look very busy (and important) if one "must" make phone
calls while driving, eat and drink breakfast while driving, read the
paper while breakfasting (and ignoring the family), have a coffee
break while texting. We get into a habit of being elsewhere mentally than where we are physically; we are never truly present to
the people and situation before us. Thanks to iPhones and similar
items, we can avoid ever "wasting" time in simple human association, in enjoying a cup of coffee or moments with a two-year-old.
It's almost a kind of Puritanism, as if enjoyment and pleasure in
others, their company, food, the view, as if all these were less worthy than work and can only be endured if accompanied by something useful.

How unlike the situation where we relish the moment before us
and try to enter as fully as possible into it, holding on to it, actually,
so as to enjoy totally a never-to-return moment. I know you get
these admonitions even on TV commercials, beer ads, etc., but
most of us still need periodic reminders that are not tied to increas-
ing our consumption of beer.

An echo of a thought found elsewhere in these lines: "From mid-life onward, the great struggle for all humans is the struggle not to give way to bitterness, resentment, self-pity and all the negativity and harsh judgments that flow from that" (Alice Miller, Swiss psychiatrist). Is it because at that age we start more seriously evaluating life and its progress that we are so tempted? Are we asking ourselves if we have gotten the love, satisfaction, recognition that we think should be our fair share? Does the tendency to self-pity and resentment build up over the years as we "collect" injuries, slights, failures, disappointments? Are we comparing ourselves to others and wondering if we have been shortchanged or passed over?

A line I've quoted elsewhere goes: "The abandonment of self-pity is the beginning of wisdom." It certainly is consonant with the Gospel for us to shrug off slights and offenses and get on with our lives and work. And it certainly seems a healthier way to live than "getting even'" or tallying up all the hurts. Starting to do that early enough might help lessen the mid-life temptation to give way to bitterness.

One expression we hear and use frequently is all too appropriate: in the dark. We say we're in the dark about someone's intentions, or I'm in the dark on that matter, or she's in the dark about what's going on. Employees complain that management leaves them in the dark about what's happening. There is often a lot of darkness, obscurity, and fogginess about what is going on in our world.

Paul says that we don't see everything clearly here and now. But believers do have some light shed on essentials. The Lord says: "I have come to the world as its light, to keep anyone who believes in me from remaining in the dark." The words and life of the Son of God do give us light on what life is for, where we're going, how we should live, what is truly of value. We know—we aren't just guessing—that honesty and trustworthiness are always good; that to love and be compassionate is never a mistake; that to do good and be generous with self is right; that God definitely loves us and wishes our good.

Our faith means that we are not in the dark about such fundamentals. The revelation of God in Christ has confirmed for us that in Jesus we see God reflected; that the Lord is my shepherd and I am in his final care. For most of us the election of the current Bishop of Rome, Francis, in 2013 has meant more awareness of the light and joy found in the Gospel.

The ancient Chinese sage Confucius put it this way: in youth we have to be on our guard against lust; in our prime against aggressiveness; in old age against greediness. Overcoming the problems of one time of our life doesn't mean we're home free. Don't worry! Something else will come along, or the old ones will return.

This is true in our prayer life too. We pray for Dad's health and comfort in old age, maybe for years; eventually, of course, he dies. For a moment we feel a blank or emptiness in our prayers. But then we hear that Jill and Ben are breaking up and our concern for them and the children drives us to pray hard again. That is resolved. But then, Jim has an inoperable malignancy. We remember him daily and more than that in prayer. And so it goes. We pray for the dead: Eternal rest grant unto them, O Lord. And very appropriately. This life gives us little rest from concern, even fears.

As Confucius suggests, there's always something to pray about, even to ask forgiveness for, some weakness that hangs in there. Even our little successes can give rise to further concern. We might make some progress, at least for a while, against our sensuality. That easily leads us to pat ourselves on the back and feel pretty self-satisfied. Another problem: self-satisfaction. The needs and concerns of our own or of those dear to us serve the great purpose of reminding us of our genuine dependence on a loving God, on grace.

Some of the "good old days" were pretty awful. Days when people who disagreed with your religious beliefs could have you beheaded; when any questioning of authority, any dissent, could lead to burning at the stake; when unanimity seems to have been prized so highly. Unity is important, of course, for a country, a church, a community. In Ephesians we read: "Make every effort to preserve the unity which has the Spirit as its origin and peace as its binding force" (4:3). Unity, however, is not the same as uniformity, unanimity. Ephesians continues: "There is but one body and one Spirit, just as there is but one hope given all of you by your call. There is one Lord, one faith, one baptism; one God and Father of all" (4:5-6).

Christians of many different stripes share much of this. At least two practical conclusions suggest themselves. One: we share much in belief and practice with our fellow Christians and should emphasize that more often. When our Methodist neighbor is crushed by sorrow, we can speak of the trust we share in God; that is more significant than our differences. Two: with fellow Catholics we also have a deep-down unity despite the fact that we must at times disagree on the implementation of Christ's teaching. Just as married couples do better to concentrate on what originally drew them together than on minor irritations, we could profitably with other Christians and fellow Catholics underline how much we have in common, above all our trust in the Lord.

Regularly we hear of celebrities sitting at the feet of a current guru; the Beatles in their day gave the late Maharishi a boost by their discipleship. It is frequent enough in our society for media personalities to speak of their "spiritual trainer," psychological or religious. Yet at the same time there is often revulsion at the idea of dependence on God or Christ. The understanding seems to be that such dependence signifies an abdication of thinking or personal responsibility, being kept in a state of childishness.

The objections to any kind of dependence are probably not very well thought through. None of us, really, is free from dependence even if it is only on the power company or the water mains. Contemporary recognition of how we and all the universe and its parts are bound together in mutual dependence should make dependence on God more understandable. Being a Christian means putting one's trust in Jesus Christ as God's word to our world, depending on him more than on any self-proclaimed wizard or preacher.

Even within the Christian faith it is important that we put our faith in God and Christ. Nothing or no one less than Christ can be the same rock-like foundation that he is. The Scriptures put it well in calling God and Christ over and over "my rock," "my refuge," "my stronghold," and "my strength." The most we, the church, the sacraments can do is point to and lead to Christ.

In my part of the world a major snowfall in March is not all that improbable. And, in itself, it's beautiful: the trees, the firs especially, are mantled in snow; the whole landscape is a clean, dazzling white. Old snow that had that dirty look is "freshened." I comment to some students on how beautiful it is. Their response indicates they think I'm being sarcastic or that I haven't looked at the calendar in a long while. They're expecting spring; they may have returned from spring break in some sunny clime . . . or they're just waiting, hoping for spring. Or, if they are seniors, their chief concern is what happens after graduation, a job or grad school. For such reasons they have no time to regard a March snowfall as beautiful! A snowfall is an unwelcome interruption of their dreams and hopes, a postponement of spring.

A good snowstorm can make for class cancellations, always welcome! Inversely, snow and ice in this part of the country make themselves very unwelcome when driving and even walking become treacherous. The snow might be beautiful, but it also brings its dangers. Much of life is this way. Delight and terror can be very close.

Reality has many facets; it affects people in many different ways. "One person's meat is another's poison" went the old truism. Everything we see or experience is colored for us by our own perspective, our own situation. A more thoroughgoing selflessness would remind us of that more often when we're tempted to pass on our own certitudes to others or ignore their contrary perception or emotional difficulties.

A man, very faithful to Sunday Mass and in fact to daily Mass, says of a woman he is courting: "She prays any place, anytime; I can't imagine praying outside of a church." Till recent decades the heavy emphasis on receiving the sacraments, Sunday Mass, and reciting certain prayers easily led some of us to thinking that there is no relationship with God apart from these "official" channels. Private, personal prayers seemed almost not to "count." Even when some intense sorrow or need came to the fore, the response often was: "Let's say an Our Father." Or, instead of trusting our own instincts, we have turned to someone else's words. Undoubtedly, many people have been driven to pray in their own words in desperate circumstances.

A bit of chapter 49 on Lent in the Rule of Benedict is apt: "During these days, therefore, we will add to the usual measure of our service something by way of private prayer." This and other measures, he says, will help us "look forward to holy Easter with joy and spiritual longing" (49.5, 7).

An established belief of all of us must be that God is everywhere, always available to hear our prayers; therefore, why not get into the habit of spending some time every day in God's presence (any place!) speaking in our own words and/or even simply sitting quietly (!) leaving our hearts and minds open to God's influence. Such prayer leads to a more comfortable relationship with God. For: "The Spirit helps us in our weakness; for we do not know how to pray as we ought, but that very Spirit intercedes with sighs too deep for words" (Rom 8:26).

Psalm 119 puts it baldly: "Before I was afflicted I strayed, but now I keep your word" (v. 67).

"Have you seen Ed lately?" a former student, Jerry, asks me. I say no. In his early twenties, Ed was handsome, played rugby, drank pretty freely, ate well, and the fellow above would describe him as a "womanizer." Well, Jerry tells me, he saw him recently. He's lost over a hundred pounds, is a vegetarian, doesn't drink, is very successful in his business. The most immediately available explanation seems to be the recent death of his mother, something he took very hard.

Another friend, bringing us up-to-date on his college classmates, says Ted is much changed for the better after a very serious accident and lives on a ranch in Utah. Bill has been sobered by the diabetes that has hit him in his thirties, has married, and seems solid compared to his wilder younger days. Energetic, always-on-the-go Joe has pulled through a very rare disease after two precarious months in a hospital; still energetic but quite a bit more focused.

One hates even to entertain the thought, but affliction, death, pain, sickness, accident, sin, all seem to be the agents of our renewal. Richard Rohr says there is no growth without one of them, though the same events can embitter and depress. There has to be some willingness to learn, to be taught, to utilize all that comes our way. "Before I was afflicted I strayed, but now I keep your word" (Ps 119:67).

"Spring still makes spring in the mind
   When sixty years are told;
Love wakes anew this throbbing heart,
   And we are never old."[33]

Ralph Waldo Emerson's recipe for youth in the heart, whatever the age, argues for some passionate interests, some enthusiasms, some loves. The context does not suggest love in the New Testament sense of charity but simply any enthusiasm that quickens the heart or brightens the eye. Some "spiritual" writers push for an end to all desires, loves, and enthusiasms so that God and love for God may be the only content of our hearts. If—as I have consistently written—God's love for us comes through the actions and words of other people, then our love for God, too, is shown through our words and actions for others, our admiration, appreciation.

To rule out all our enthusiasms and loves as hostile to the love of God makes an artificial division and insinuates that all that sparks our love or interest is evil. Appreciation and love for what is beautiful or attractive is no sin. It is, in fact, the proper evaluation of what God has made. God saw that it was all good, Genesis tells us; why shouldn't we?

What a change! From being an oft-persecuted sect, Christianity had become by 380 CE a state religion. It became fashionable to be a Christian; it was a way to advancement. Laws were made to promote the faith. It all sounded good to many Christians and such an arrangement continued in many places till modern times. Unfortunately, this often meant that Christians did not feel personal responsibility for their faith. Being a Christian was more a matter of where you were born than of genuine personal commitment. Believers depended on laws to enforce Christian belief and morals. The temptation to do that is still with us. When people aren't convinced of the Christian stand on a moral issue, there are always some who think making it into law would help.

The brief parable of Jesus about how a small amount of yeast is able to permeate and transform a large amount of flour suggests a better way to influence our society than by laws (Matt 13:31-35). People who believe in God's love can spread that by quiet lives of faithfulness, joy, and genuine love. Observation tells us again and again how powerful individual example can be—how people are led to Christ not by argument, force, and talk but by good example. The life of Christ in his members, nourished at the Eucharist, makes this example possible.

"Anyone who is not against us is with us" (Mark 9:40). That's quite different from saying that whoever is not with us is against us. The words of Jesus here tell us to accept all those who do good, who work to better the world, who serve others, who cooperate in combating the power of greed and exploitation, of hatred and prejudice. The important thing in the long run is not whether good action is labeled Catholic, Christian, or Buddhist, but whether, like the deeds of Jesus, it does good for poor, suffering humans.

Although the teaching and example of Jesus are powerful in motivating people to the service of others, it remains true that there are many who, without accepting that teaching, put to shame those of us who claim it. God's grace works in many places and under many names. Jesus told those disciples shocked at a man not of their company who was expelling demons in his name: "Do not try to stop him" (Mark 9:39).

We should rejoice in the good and cooperate with those who do it. It might encourage us or challenge us to continue the good we do or to more generosity. If all the good things being done for the poor and suffering around us are being done by others, why or how are we failing? What we do and celebrate at our worship together, our solidarity with Christ and each other, that must show itself beyond the church doors.

Complaints about the institutional church are standard and often understandable. They usually go: "I believe in God or Christ, and I find God in people, in nature; I don't need any church or formal service." We have had for centuries much emphasis on hierarchy, organization, and buildings, to the neglect of faith and individual responsibility. The initiative and the contributions of laypeople were minimized or ignored. We still too often wait for "Father" or the bishop or the pope to act.

Jesus encourages more initiative by ordinary Christians when he says: "Where two or three are gathered in my name, there am I in their midst" (Matt 18:20). They don't have to be gathered in the church or as Catholics or Lutherans. "We are the church." The baptized are the body of Christ in this world. The responsibility for the Christian faith belongs to all of us; hierarchy, dioceses, boards, conferences, etc., should not steal our thunder.

In this same context Jesus speaks of prayer: "If you join your voices on earth to pray for anything whatever, it shall be granted you by my Father in heaven" (Matt 18:19). This is certainly an area where Catholics and other Christians might easily join or those who simply believe in God might join in times of tragedy or difficulty. And fortunately, we do hear of Christians of various denominations consoling and helping each other; of believers of all religions—Muslims, Jews, Hindus, Christians—turning to God together in times of disaster. But there are times when we Christians seem to be waiting for someone "higher up" to speak or act when we have that ability and duty by our baptism and often also by our education and skill.

We think of problems with marriage and fidelity as typical of our time. And, given the fact that people live so much longer today, maybe these problems are more prevalent. But listen to the response of the disciples to Jesus after hearing him underline the indissolubility of marriage: "If that is the case between man and wife, it is better not to marry" (Matt 19:3-12).

They evidently approve of and are used to the possibility of divorce as it existed among them. To hear Jesus' severely uncompromising words about the indissolubility of marriage (with one exception) strikes them as too tough. "How could anyone enter into marriage if there was no out?" they think. Their remarks tell us a lot about how far Jesus had to bring them to accept his teaching. It also underlines how difficult faithfulness and commitment have always been.

For much of recorded history, there have been problems with fidelity and commitment. Our times might glorify the uncommitted state but the issue is older. What does it all say to us? That we should despair of the possibility? That we should accept disintegrating marriages as the norm? Obviously, Jesus presents a permanent union as the ideal. This teaching implies that any commitment we've made requires a daily renewal; it cannot be taken for granted. In the Eucharist we have put before us the supreme example of commitment: "He loved his own even to death on a cross." Through genuine participation in that cross and death, we gain the strength to live out our commitments, to husband or wife, to children, to job, to neighbors and friends, to God.

What can illness teach? Patience. Or, at least it can if we're open to learning from such an experience. A young man who had surgery for a cancerous brain tumor says that after his first surgery (with his scalp partly shaved), he went to the college library; a few friends greeted him warmly, but: "Most of my acquaintances in the room quickly turned and hid behind their computers, acting as if they hadn't even seen me. Hiding was a reaction I received a lot over the year (of treatment), but I have to say that I was initially quite shocked by this."

Shocked and probably hurt. Along with the pain and distress of cancer, you hardly need to have friends seem to turn from you. He found his male friends singularly unable to deal with his cancer. Visits from them were few and far between. Men seem more afraid of illness than women. Or they are afraid it could be them next: "Maybe if I avoid the sick person, I can avoid anything similar." They're worried about what to say, not realizing that just the presence of a familiar face, the touch of a hand, would be welcome.

The same fellow records how pleasing it was when a couple of male friends did stop by: "We talked about movies, basketball, the weather, and their lives rather than mine. It was so refreshing to hear about life outside of my dark little world."

"What has been, that will be; what has been done, that will be done. Nothing is new under the sun" (Eccl 1:9). This certainly unprogressive view is but a part of the seemingly hopeless tone of the Hebrew Scripture's book of Ecclesiastes. It very likely resonates with our mood at times, though we'd be in tough shape if it were continual. Our activities, life itself, seem empty. The opening verses of Ecclesiastes say just that: "Vanity of vanities! All things are vanity!" A more contemporary translation would say: emptiness, emptiness; everything is empty. Every line in this melancholy book echoes in us at some time or other. There are times when nothing seems to satisfy; the most pleasant experiences leave us asking, "Is that all there is?"

This book of Ecclesiastes, so unusual in the Bible, has its place. It tells us that our desolate moods and feelings are understandable; our doubts and queries are also not unusual; others have had them. It should give us more patience with ourselves and sympathy for others who feel emptiness. We don't just slap them on the back and say, "Cheer up!" We can't know the burdens that afflict them. Our own good cheer, discreetly shown, practical help, and prayer are all good approaches to the misery of others. For ourselves, to hang on to some word of prayer, even if it reproaches God, is sometimes the best we can do. As Ecclesiastes says later (chap. 3): "There is a time and a season for every matter under the sun. . . . A time to weep, and a time to laugh; a time to mourn, and a time to dance."

A young man writes shortly before his wedding: "It's so wonderful being loved by Kate. How could I ever deserve this? Why me? I'm so grateful." Much more readily we ask, "Why me?" when disaster or tragedy hits; we even feel at times as if God is singling us out for hard treatment. The diverse responses suggest yet another way of dividing human beings into two categories: (1) those who look at everything as a gift, with gratitude and appreciation; and (2) those who see the universe and God as owing them all they have and a lot more. The different attitudes are largely the result of a decision, unconscious or otherwise, on our part. At least, there seems to be room here for us to exercise such a choice.

The atmosphere of the Mass or Lord's Supper is one of thanksgiving; that's why traditionally it is called Eucharist after the Greek word for thanksgiving. In the texts of the Mass we hear and breathe this expansive spirit: "Let us give thanks to the Lord our God." "It is right and just." "It is truly right and just, our duty and our salvation, / always and everywhere to give you thanks, / Lord, holy Father, almighty and eternal God, / through Christ our Lord."[34]

Henri Nouwen says that because gratitude is not always such an obvious attitude toward life, Jesus gave us the Eucharist to enable us "to choose gratitude instead of resentment and hope instead of despair."[35]

"There is an appointed time for everything, and a time for every affair under the heavens. A time to be born, and a time to die; . . . a time to be silent, and a time to speak . . ." (Eccl 3:1-10). This famous passage expresses an attitude that is fairly rare in Scripture. It suggests resignation, acceptance of what is, of the inevitability of birth and death, war and peace, laughing and weeping, even love and hate.

More often in Scripture we meet encouragement to do something about bad things; we see the Savior continually healing people. In

Matthew's Gospel, Peter meets Jesus' announcement of his coming passion and death by saying he will never allow it. Even Jesus' first words at the time of his passion were a request that if possible, he could be spared what was coming. We admire and propose that attitude more often than resignation.

But there are moments in human life when the words of Ecclesiastes offer some comfort and even strength. We have struggled, exhausted every conceivable measure to better a situation. There comes a moment when we do best to accept what is. There might be a time to be silent, a time to mourn. The Lord himself finally prayed in the garden to the Father, "but thy will, not mine be done." And on the cross, "Father, into your hands I commend my spirit." "There is an appointed time for everything."

At times we Christians have spoken of self-denial, the cross, as if it were some kind of choice we had to make among a bewildering number of possibilities. But the real crosses don't have to be looked for; they come. They are an inevitable part of every life. It seems pretty certain that we will all at some time be close to feeling like Job. Why was I born? Why should I live? Our happiness, our hopes are dashed to the ground by an accident that happens to a family member, by a disease that kills a child or parent, by some terrible disappointment in our work or another person, by crushing loneliness or boredom. They make us cry out like our Lord: "My God, why have you forsaken me?" (Mark 15:34).

These are the genuine crosses; nothing we choose can equal the ones given to us by life and our circumstances. The suffering and death of Jesus came about not because he wanted them but because he had chosen a good life and a mission from God. He was to feel the consequences in the ill will that caused. We all face both people and situations that are hostile and about which we can do nothing.

This is probably the most heroic thing we can do: accept what comes from the unchangeable circumstances and people of our life, what faithfulness to our responsibilities asks from us, the inconveniences and boredom of everyday life. That is where we above all find the crucified—and risen Lord.

Psalm 22:1 reads: "My God, my God, why have you forsaken me?" and verse 11: "Do not leave me alone. . . . For there is no one to help." Any suffering or pain is more than sufficient for most of us. But the opening cry of this psalm, which Jesus quotes on the cross (Mark 15:34), and the other verse in the same psalm add another note that only deepens suffering: feeling alone, abandoned, forgotten; with no one to help, to offer a friendly touch, to mumble a few consoling words; no one to simply be present—this seems the final blow.

Many of us with any experience of visiting the sick, the suffering, or the dying realize that at times the most we can do is simply be with the person, words showing how inadequate they can be. Retired physician J. Weston Smith, sharing by his presence the pains of his ailing and elderly wife, writes in his poem "As Much as I Love Her":

As much as I love her,
I can't feel her pain:
I can offer only sympathy.

As much as I love her,
I can't heal her wounds:
I can offer only sympathy.

As much as I love her,
I can't swallow for her:
I can offer only sympathy.

As much as I love her,
I have to realize that
even though we've reunited
in life,

We leave earthly life as
we arrived,
alone.

Again, simply being with her, with him, maybe stumbling through a spur-of-the-moment prayer is often the best we can do. Those few who stood by the Lord on Calvary were mute—but present.

Early on as Bishop of Rome, Benedict XVI said that his task was "to make the light of Christ shine before men and women," not his own light but that of Christ.[36] Similarly, some decades earlier John XXIII hoped that the Vatican Council would clear away all that obscured the light of Christ's face. In John's Gospel, Jesus says: "I came into the world as light, so that everyone who believes in me might not remain in darkness" (John 12). We pray in one of the psalms: "Your word is a light for my path." The "word" is both Scripture and the Lord who is the word. Through his life and teaching, he sheds light on the confusion that obscures our direction and decisions. His light and life do not so much give us a collection of intellectual certainties as they give a deep assurance in the midst of sin, suffering, and sorrow.

John Henry Newman memorably traces the response we should develop in a poem, "The Pillar of the Cloud." Our trust in Christ the light leaves the details of life's journey to God's loving care, rather than asking for a blueprint.

Newman writes:

Lead, Kindly Light, amid the encircling gloom
    Lead Thou me on!
The night is dark, and I am far from home—
    Lead Thou me on!
Keep Thou my feet; I do not ask to see
The distant scene,—one step enough for me.

A bit later he tells us it took him some time to come to this total trust:

I was not ever thus, nor pray'd that Thou
    Shouldst lead me on.
I lov'd to choose and see my path; but now
    Lead Thou me on![37]

"We brought nothing into this world, nor have we the power to take anything out. If we have food and clothing we have all that we need" (1 Tim 6:7-8). "You can't take it with you" goes the old saw, but the letter to Timothy goes a step further and reminds us that "you didn't bring it with you" either. Earlier the writer speaks of being content with a sufficiency (v. 6). A good number of people today, even apart from New Testament teaching, see the dangers in being dominated by consumerism—the desire to have, accumulate, and consume things.

An uncluttered life and environment leaves us free for more important elements of human life: the company of other people, of our family, friendship, conversation, contemplation, prayer, reading. Human life is "human" when it is centered more on our fellow human beings than on things. We become more fully human in interaction with other people. When we fall for the lure of things, new gadgets, new stuff, we easily become their prisoners.

Any movement toward the more simple life is counter to the major drives of our society. And it takes some conviction and strong beliefs to resist the pull of our world of things and their accumulation. The real treasures, riches, are within our personalities and human nature, in life close to God and our human neighbors.

Anyone living in or visiting one of our big cities encounters beggars, the poor and homeless, street people. They are often divided into the deserving and the undeserving, though it doesn't seem to be a distinction Jesus ever made. Typically, they are teenage girls with plaintive voices, hardened old guys with all their belongings in a plastic bag or a shopping cart, occasionally a mother and children. Some carry signs indicating they have AIDS or that they are Iraq veterans. Amid the charm and exuberant life of the city they remind us of the injustices and inequalities of life, even if we grant an occasional suspicion that some are hoaxes.

In the midst of our comfort, it's good for us to be reminded of this and of how well off we are, no matter how sorry we feel for ourselves at times. Virgilio Elizondo writes: "The role of the powerless is to evangelize the powerful."[38] Whether they say anything or not, like Lazarus they lie or stand outside our homes and businesses, pricking our consciences. They tell us that all is not well. They also preach generosity to us. Figures on charitable giving in our country show that the poor give more proportionally than do the wealthy. Stories abound, too, of how the poor are so willing to share.

"Stay with us. It is nearly evening" (Luke 24:29). Two disciples speak the words to Jesus in chapter 24 of Luke. At the moment the two have not yet recognized that Jesus had been walking with them. Shortly after, while they are at table, and when they see Jesus break the bread, they recognize him.

This beautiful story suggests many things. One is that Jesus, risen, is not with them or anyone as he was during his earthly existence, but that he continues to be with us in the Lord's Supper and in the community of the believers. The fact that they walked alongside him earlier in the story without recognizing him tells us that the Lord might be met, served, and loved in unlikely people on our journey through life. That their hearts were "burning inside" when he talked to them tells us, too, that he is present in the impact of Scripture.

We can go further and remind ourselves that celebrating his presence with ordinary bread and wine at a table assures us that his risen presence is with us most clearly as we share life, time, and all we have and are with others. We need not look for visions in the sky or only in the Eucharistic host while overlooking his presence in ordinary life, in its sorrows and joys, its magnificence and its lowliness. The crises that darken our lives especially urge us to call out, "Stay with us. It is nearly evening." Easter, in one of its many facets, is about the always-available presence, in crises and in joy, of the Risen Christ.

The funeral of a young woman murdered by an intruder in her apartment prompts many questions and frustrations along with great sadness among her friends. Two of Sandy's passions were music and children; she taught in a local school and loved her guitar. Friends and preachers both know how inadequate words are at such times. In Peter De Vries's novel *The Blood of the Lamb*, the father of a young girl who has died of leukemia says that in the end all we can do is sit side-by-side on "the mourners' bench"

holding each other in silence, linked by grief and compassion. No matter how poorly, how inadequately, we must express ourselves even in unspeakable sadness.

Another clue about what we can do comes from Sandy's passion for music. In it, whether performing or listening, we often find an outlet for thoughts and feelings too deep for banal words. The disaffected often pooh-pooh religious services, but the shared experience of music, as well as our poor words, is, I suspect, for most people some help and a necessity. Aldous Huxley writes: "After silence, that which comes nearest to expressing the inexpressible is music."[39]

You might say that even God felt the inadequacy of words when he resorted to something fleshly and palpable. God's word, God's son, became flesh (John 1:14). Rather than attempting to give us some verbal explanation for suffering and tragedy, God has shown solidarity with us in suffering by the cross and death of Jesus. There is God's answer to the age-old human question "Why me? Why did this happen?" "My Son wasn't spared; you should not be too surprised."

Faith in the resurrection of Jesus is not based on the testimony of a bunch of gullible people. Mark tells us what a skeptical reception Mary Magdalene got when she tried to tell the disciples about seeing the risen Lord: "When they heard that he was alive and had been seen by her, they refused to believe it" (16:11). Similarly with the disciples who said they had met Jesus walking to Emmaus: "The others put no more faith in them than in Mary Magdalene" (16:13). The resurrection was not something psychologically convenient for the disciples, but something forced on them by reality and repeated testimony.

It is encouraging that all the evidence in the Gospels indicates how slow and uncomprehending the disciples were during his lifetime about who Jesus was. And, all the more, this should help us in our doubts. Some of our prayer should be for a firmer, more genuine faith in the risen Lord and all that this means for human misery and death. The joy that echoes in the prayer of the church and in the music of the season can be truly ours if we recall and ponder the resistance of the disciples to the resurrection and how they came to believe.

We are prevented at times from doing good by thinking, "What I can do is so insignificant; why bother? It will change nothing." We too readily leave it all to the shakers and movers. Even in our religion this is reinforced by the attention we give to the great saints or even simply to a pope or bishop. Spotlighting the saints' accomplishments certainly helps us realize how we should respond to God, but Jesus speaks in various parables of how the kingdom grows from the smallest of beginnings. We can have faith that even the little things we do are worth doing; they have an impact. (See, for example, the parables of the mustard seed and the yeast: Luke 13:18-21.)

The lives of us ordinary human beings are of value even if we never make canonization (a pretty arbitrary process) or the cover of *People* magazine or the evening news. The two parables remind us that minute beginnings can lead to large, important results. Instead of regretting that we can't help all the homeless in Mumbai or New York, why not do something to better the situation where we live: in Cape Town, Juarez, or Bristol? Instead of regretting that we can't have the impact of some TV preacher, we can make our own environment—the home, the job—a more hopeful place for others by our comments, our attitude. Instead of admiring those who suffer terrible things for goodness and God, we can exhibit patience with the little irritations of our own lives.

All of us together, trying to live by the example of the Lord, are a leaven that helps transform the world. That endless fountain of hope Pope Francis says in a TED talk: "Let us help each other, all together, to remember that the other is not a statistic or a number. The other has a face. The 'you' is always a real presence, a person to take care of. . . . [Let us] use our hands and our heart to comfort the other, to take care of those in need."[40]

It rightly seems tragic to us well-off first worlders that the wretchedly poor we see on our television screens must spend every available moment scratching out an existence. We think of ourselves as so free of that. But are we? In speaking about his return, Jesus says that it will be like it was in the days of Noah: "They ate and drank, they took husbands and wives, right up to the day Noah entered the ark—and when the flood came, it destroyed them all" (Luke 17:26-37). Most of our time is absorbed in eating and drinking, sleeping, planting, taking husbands and wives, building, buying and selling. These things not only absorb our time but easily also our energy. The tone of Jesus' words is that we are in danger of being too bound to all these activities, good in themselves. In a way, we are hardly in a position all that different from the very poor.

We have so much and yet we still push ourselves to have more and more, to more absorption in all these activities. Jesus tells us to take all this a little less seriously and to leave some space and time for attention to the end and the world to come. The end, whether of our world or our lives, will come in the midst of the ordinary pursuits of daily life. Definitely, they are not wrong in themselves; it's only that we need to keep them in perspective, not allow ourselves to be drowned in them. There should be time in our lives for each other, for God, for prayer and reflection, for worship, for silence, even for so-called useless things like poetry, games, music and dancing. Possibly those of us who do take time for these things have an obligation to witness to this in our public lives.

"I will bless the Lord at all times, his praise always on my lips" (Ps 34:1). The devout couple who just came back from a pilgrimage only to discover that their twenty-year-old son had a malignant tumor could be excused for choosing another mantra. And the mother, the more vocal of the two, did ask why and express her impotent disappointment with God. Dad quietly sat alongside her, held her, and tried to comfort her. The psalm goes on to say that the Lord sets us free from all our terrors, rescues the poor and the distressed. "Those who revere the Lord lack nothing, their appeals are heard. They are happy who seek refuge in him." The couple mentioned above and their son can be forgiven for having trouble with these sentiments.

Most of us will in some way or on some day be in similar straits. How can or will we bless or praise the Lord at such times? Many of the biblical writers before Christ expected that vindication and rescue would be sure here and now for those who trusted in God. We can share their joyful trust if we allow that our favorable response from the Lord might (1) come otherwise than we expect or (2) beyond this life.

The experience of the saints—and among them are many of our family members and friends—is the surest warranty we have for believing that trust in God is never misplaced. These are people who have learned by prolonged trust even amid terrors and trials that the Lord hears and cares. Therefore, "I will bless the Lord at all times, his praise always on my lips."

"But I arise in the morning, torn between a desire to improve (or save) the world and a desire to enjoy (or savor) the world. This makes it hard to plan the day" (E. B. White)![41] There are those who wake up every day determined to save the world; we recognize them by their earnestness and concentration. And there are those bent solely on savoring or enjoying the world too. They can be childlike or thoughtless, or they can be adults who value the present more than most of us can manage.

Sharing E. B. White's feeling might be more typical and, as he says, it makes for a tension that carries through much of our activity. Each of us must work out her/his own balance; no one else can quite know the circumstances and drives of our life. Perhaps we can test how we balance saving the world and enjoying the world by the effects on those around us. Are we more responsive to spouse, family, friends? Perhaps saving and enjoying will coincide at times.

All too clearly and frequently in terms of physicality, we come full circle in our lives. The dependence and weakness of infancy once again seems to be our lot in old age. Someone else has to clean us up or clean up after us, augment our mobility, and it can get worse. . . . A lot of this is not very attractive to any of us, but the abdication of competitiveness and aggression, an increased tolerance of human foibles, these are more admirable qualities that age can foster.

Our Lord and much religious and mystical tradition see the ideal of human development to be a recovery of the simplicity and lack of self-consciousness of the infant. Only this time it can be willingly and freely chosen. A French poet wrote this: "Genius is merely childhood recalled at will" (Baudelaire).[42] For our purposes, we could alter it to read: "True discipleship is childhood recaptured freely by acceptance of God's grace."

The writer of the book of Proverbs asks: "Give me neither poverty nor riches" (30:7). Either one can be very hard on the human spirit. For sure most of us are more frightened of poverty than we are of riches. In fact, superficially riches don't seem to be such a bad idea after all. We could use a little more leeway in our income; we could enjoy not having to scrimp; we'd like to be able to pay off that mortgage and see a little more theater or games in the new stadium or take that trip to Aruba.

The author of Proverbs has an even-handed approach. He says: "If I have too much I am liable to ignore God and say to myself, 'I guess I'm in charge. I don't need anyone else. I might not even need God since I am able to provide for my own security.'" On the other hand, he says: "If I have too little, there is real danger that I shall pant after what I do not have or, further, scheme to get it from someone who has." Our newspapers and media show us almost daily a host of contemporary perils of poverty and abundance. Overall the dangers related to having or not having material things come from our attitude, our desires, not from the things themselves. Nothing God has made is evil.

Seeking signs, miracles, is seemingly as old as the human race. Jesus says: "This is an evil age. It seeks a sign" (Luke 11:29). Despite the particular situation in which he spoke these words, they sound timeless: we still look for signs. Someone says the face of Jesus has appeared on a fridge door and crowds tie up traffic to get there. Others expect some vision of Mary to supplement the Gospels and tell us the exact time of the end of things. But all the while there are signs and messages being addressed to us in everyday life to which we have become insensitive. In both the suffering and deprivation of some and in the goodness, kindness, and generosity of others.

If we walk down the sidewalks of any large city, we are sure to see street people and other sad cases dotting the way. We have, we do become, hardened to all this. Our TV brings us news stories of war, genocide, starvation, terrible crimes, and we don't cry. Our movies are often built around killing after killing, which becomes—incredible as it is to say—entertainment. We become immune to the impact of poverty, crime, and war. Aren't these signs to us? Can we reawaken our sensitivity somehow? Can we at least bring crime, poverty, and war before God in prayer and thus show some concern, show that we've got the message? Signs, even miracles, are all around us.

Whether it's the harried man or woman who has spent the whole day with energetic and lovable, but very noisy, little children; or someone who has been involved in an ongoing struggle for months; or someone caught in the midst of irrational war or terrorism—"I'd just like a little peace" is the likely wish. Peace, the word sums up the most profound desire of many a human being. Yet, in any obvious sense, it is pretty elusive. When it does break out in our world, we all know it's only a matter of days till we'll hear about another conflict.

Yet the Gospel of John has the nerve, one might almost say, to put these words on the lips of Jesus: "'Peace' is my gift to you" (14:27).

If peace here is not simply some bit of airy sentiment, it must mean more than meets the eye. The words appear in the context of a long address before the passion and death of Jesus where the victory of Jesus is also promised. His words and his resurrection are the basis of peace for the believer. That peace does not mean the end of all unpleasantness and conflict but a deep reassurance, way below the surface of agitation and hatred. It is a confidence that we will overcome, that the Risen Victor over death and all ills is with us. It is not that Arab and Jew have become buddies or that the street gang and the police are united for the good of the neighborhood. We must certainly hope for and work for that. But what the Lord promises is more a profound sense of trust and quiet built on the certainty of God's love and its final triumph. Possibly that can live deep in our hearts despite the din and clangor of life around us.

What is revealed to the world in Jesus Christ is, in one sense, nothing new. What is new is the dramatic expression in a living human being who shared our life, suffered, died, and rose again. God did not just begin to love human beings when Jesus was born or only love them in Palestine. God has always loved creation and everything in it. The refrain in the first chapter of Genesis is that God looked on everything in creation and saw that it was good. We can see the apparently tough approach God took with Israel as like the regulations parents use with growing children. God has never really changed the message; it has always been that God loves us and wills what is best for us, is with us. The packaging has been different depending on our receptivity or maturity.

In Luke's Jesus, in the great Jewish prophets and in the apostles, we hear proclaimed one great assurance for all of us. We are not abandoned; evil, sin, disease, war, and death do not have the last word. In the death and resurrection of Jesus, in his whole life, in fact, we see how far God's love for us has gone. Even elsewhere in another religion, in the great religious book of India, the Bhagavad Gita, the god Krishna seems to witness to something similar speaking to his followers: "Listen to my words, for you are precious to me. . . . Keep your mind on me, be my devotee—you will come to me, I promise, for you are dear to me" (18:64-65). God is with us and for us; in a particularly concrete way the Eucharist assures us of that. Maybe there are inklings of that love in other world religions . . . ?

Trust in God, another word for faith in much of the Scriptures, is not based on the extraordinary knowledge we have of God's mind. Trust is based on what we know of the life and message of Jesus and, above all, that God raised him from the dead. God's love for us, and our faith and hope in God, are justified in Jesus who shows us how total is God's love. God intends, Jesus tells us, to do the same for us: rescue us from suffering, disappointment, and death.

In the midst of his terrible suffering, the loss of family and everything he and his family owned, Job retains a similar trust in God. He says, "I know that my Vindicator lives" (Job 19:25). The words in an older translation are set to moving music by Handel in the *Messiah*: "I know that my Redeemer liveth." Living before Jesus, Job had no such vivid picture as we have of God's love for us but still, on the basis of what God had done for his people over the centuries, Job was able to say that he trusted God to deliver him. In the Eucharist we are close to God's love and mercy in the presence of Christ in the bread and wine, in God's word, and in each other. "I know that my Vindicator, my Redeemer lives."

"Since you have been raised up in the company with Christ, be intent on things above rather than on things on earth. After all, you have died! Your life is hidden now with Christ in God" (Col 3:1-2). Believing by our faith and baptism that the Risen Christ is already living in and operative in us is the framework within which Christians can see the less appetizing facts of life. If we are sorrowing because of enduring disagreements in the family, pain and illness, financial difficulties, Colossians encourages us. We read there how a deep-down confidence that our life is in God will enable us to live through this. If our faith makes others ignore us or consider us out of touch, even attack us, that is all a sharing in the cross of Christ, which precedes a full resurrection.

Being risen with Christ, in other words, is no simple cure-all for serious, even desperate human situations. But it encourages us to hope and trust that God does not mean this desperate situation to be the end, that God can, with the available human resources, help us through this, even bring good from it. Faith in Christ and his risen life in us do not take us out of the mess and misery of human life. It offers us a way through all this with hope and strength. Celebrating Christ's presence at the Eucharist under the forms of such simple things as bread and wine reminds us that even amid the agony, discouragement, and drudgery of daily life we have God-given strength for facing them.

We know, Karl Rahner wrote, that the Holy Spirit is effectively working in us "when one dares to pray in silence and darkness and knows that he is heard."[43] The first part of that phrase must express the almost universal experience of believers: we pray, we turn to God without sensing God's touch or encouragement. How else do most of us pray? Prayer is fundamentally an exercise of turning to God for help or in thanksgiving without having the usual human accompaniments of seeing anything or hearing any voice. What Rahner suggests that may be indicative of the Spirit's work in us is the assurance that we are heard. In other words, prayer presupposes at least a bit of faith. Prayer in pure desperation may be more heavy on hope than assurance.

The advance in Rahner's statement is that we pray and know that God hears us. That is what makes us continue to pray when nothing seems to change, when the cancer persists in our spouse, when the unemployment continues, when the mental pain is still there. Those who have discontinued prayer or never seriously made it a part of their lives often seem dissuaded by just this essential aspect of prayer: we speak to and trust a being who seldom if ever speaks in return. The Holy Spirit is working in us—we know we have some beginning of faith—when we keep on praying and know that we are heard. Only time and experience can bring us the Holy Spirit's assurance and a response of God's making.

Porcupines huddle together in order to avoid freezing, but stand far enough apart to ensure that none of them is pricked on another's quill (Arthur Schopenhauer). For us, this would be minimal civility. But say we've just had a painful argument or are in a bad mood and the phone rings. Most of us will not snap at the caller with some testy "Whadduyawant?" If we are used to some basic civility, we at least mutter an "Hello" or "This is Bill Smith."

Civility is not the love that Christ commands, but it may be the beginning or possibly a consequence of it. One of many definitions is that civility consists in the "'supportive interchanges,' the little rituals through which we acknowledge that we are connected to others, even if only by our shared humanity: we signal our awareness of the connection by acknowledging it" (quoted by Henry Hitchings).[44] Louis Armstrong sings:

> I see friends shaking hands. Saying, "How do you do?" They're really saying, "I love you."[45]

Even if we don't see these customs as romantic "love," they can express basic regard for other human beings.

Bonjour, Buenos días, How do you do? What's shakin?—these greetings are civility, customs which rein in our feelings and treat other human beings as worthy of respect. Once internalized, such customs operate independently of our feelings. When we greet others, we recognize that they, too, were created by this same God, have God's "breath" in them. The Hindu greeting *Namaste* says it well: "I bow to the God within you." Regular use of such conventions enables us to go beyond our feelings at the moment to honor and respect the other. Used frequently enough, they can even mean that we put others ahead of ourselves and of our moods. Such simple rituals tell me that how I feel should not be the prime consideration in my relations with other people. All this is getting pretty close to the love that Christ commands us to show every human being.

Ryan is a lively, somewhat impish, college sophomore. Wrestling provides some outlet for his energy and feistiness. His friends one day insist that he show his tattoo. It turns out to be a tiger, ready to pounce, on his upper arm. Typically, he explains to this Catholic priest, "We Lutherans get one of these with baptism." (Would that be the equivalent of that indelible mark we talk about?) From the reactions of other parents, I'm sure his might be somewhat chagrined by this.

We older and more thoughtful people always think of the long term: will he still want this when he's fifty? At least there is some consolation that it is not a heart encircled with words: "Forever it belongs to Angie." Protestations of undying love are often premature for college sophomores. We can't undo totally the mistakes or imprudence of youth; at most we can forget them a bit, expect others to forgive, move on. There is no way of getting through adolescence and youth without some allowance for mistakes, no way of getting through life itself without this.

For many of us setting off on a trip, even an easy one, is exciting, often to the point of making sleep difficult the night before. The poet W. H. Auden says that before any significant journey, we really imagine ourselves as the great hero "setting off in search of an enchanted princess or the Waters of Life."[46] We are much more likely to refer to life as a journey or voyage than as a bouquet or meal or garden. The journey image fits with our effort to understand life, to find our purpose. The story of the Israelites' wanderings in the desert before getting to the Promised Land (Exodus) always suggests comparisons to our own life. Like them, we're often afraid of the next stage; we, too, would rather stay put than grow; we grumble and complain; we're confused and fearful of the future. Though this might be true of all of us at some point in life, it's especially the case with young people confused and worried about the future, family, friends, finances, faith. Those of us who believe that the answer to many of our questions is found in the teaching of Jesus might need patience with those, whether younger or not, who don't see that so clearly.

The young, possibly our own children, need space to move, even to make mistakes, and they need patience and love from parents, teachers, clergy. Those who have been on the journey longer and have reached some certainties might have to restrain themselves from passing on all those certainties to the young at one time. Because we think we know how life should be lived doesn't mean it is always helpful to pour it all into ears and hearts that aren't ready for it. We might all be going in the same direction, but there are a lot of different ways of doing it. Our patience and gentleness with the less sure might be the most effective help we give them.

"Isn't this the carpenter, the son of Mary, a brother of James and Joses and Judas and Simon? Aren't his sisters our neighbors here?" (Mark 6:3). These are the words of people in Jesus' "own part of the country." They are a way of whittling down the importance of Jesus. In other words, they say, would any exceptional person come from this neighborhood? It seems to be an enduring characteristic of us humans.

We spend our time (before the TV) and our adulation on overpaid commercial athletes and neglect the hard-playing, hard-working boys and girls next door. We look for heroic Christians somewhere across the world or in history and miss the ones we live or work with right here. It's shocking that TV evangelists get incredible financial support from viewers while local congregations and pastors struggle and beg. (As someone has pointed out, the TV evangelist won't be visiting you when you're laid up with cancer. The local pastor and church workers are the ones who will be there.)

Support and encouragement of our neighbors in their work, sport, lives, talents, achievements is so often neglected in favor of celebrities. The little people—those around us who are doing good work, living good lives—they need and deserve support and appreciation. The big guns will get theirs as well as outsized salaries. Recognizing the talent and goodness near us also builds community, solidarity. Is not this what we mean when we say that charity and many good things all begin at home?

"Rejoice, O young man, while you are young and let your heart be glad in the days of your youth. Remember your creator in the days of your youth, before the evil days come" (Eccl 11:9–12:8). In this section of his book, Ecclesiastes speaks of the pains of old age, again, as we come to expect from him, with melancholy. This might have been sharpened for him by the uncertainty and lack of hope he and his contemporaries had about afterlife. While poets have spoken of how the best was yet to come—in old age, that is—many an aging person has felt more like Ecclesiastes. The best has been.

The author speaks of the years to come when one will say, "I have no pleasure in them." He lists the hazards of old age: failing sight and hearing, shaky limbs: "One fears heights and perils in the street." Those kids racing by on skateboards, the too-quickly changing traffic lights. As so often, Ecclesiastes by its presence in the Bible gives us permission to feel some dread about aging, even some irritation. For most of us, old age, if it means anything new, means new pains, new ills, new difficulties even as we might enjoy other aspects. Experience shows us what good God can draw out of the pains and worries of old age. What generosity and kindness one's old age can bring forth in the young and healthy. United to Christ in baptism and the Eucharist, we share in the power that transformed his pain and death into joy and resurrection.

By now it's a cliché: knowledge doesn't save, faith and love do. But there is still a great place for knowledge in the living of Christian faith today. Though it cannot replace prayer and practice, it can help our growth and perspective. A detail mentioned only in passing in Luke 4:38 is an example of the broadening power of some knowledge, especially of Scripture itself and of history: "On leaving the synagogue, Jesus entered the house of Simon. Simon's mother-in-law was in the grip of a severe fever." Simon is, of course, the man later called Peter by Jesus. The most important of the apostles and their spokesman, a future martyr in Rome, the man Catholic Christians see as the nearest thing to what we have for some centuries called the pope, this man was married.

For some time in the Catholic Church it has been expected that clergy be unmarried, unlike the earliest followers of Jesus. Knowledge of the history and development of the Christian faith shows us how customs and practices have changed. It gives us a broader perspective on current debates within the church. An African saying goes: "He who never leaves home thinks his mother is the only cook." Our time and place or some other favorite century, say the nineteenth, these are, obviously, not the final standards for what can and cannot be in Christian practice. More knowledge can help us develop well-based convictions and preserve us from thinking that today's model is the only one. Christ is the same today, yesterday, and tomorrow but much else can change.

The fellow is tending the coffee shop counter. We start talking about the interest and beauty of the city. It comes up that I am in the city for a month, part of my sabbatical. What do I teach, he asks? I answer him by saying it's something unusual, you might never have heard of. He says, "Theology?" I'm amazed at his guess; has decades of teaching Theology so marked—or disfigured—my face? He says he took several courses in World Religions, Old Testament in college. Very interested in theology. He adds: "I'll have to ask you some tough theological questions before you leave." I say: "Oh, oh, maybe I better get the check." He gets it for me and says very sincerely: "Give me a bit of wisdom, something to think about."

I recall a line from a writer who, as a child of ten, had discovered the murdered body of his mother. Asked in later years about how he has coped with this, he said, as if to distill his wisdom: "The abandonment of self-pity is the beginning of wisdom." I give him this. He says: "Wow, that fits me right now!" (He feels a BA should mean more than work as a barista.)

Before I leave, he asks me to repeat the phrase. I do; he writes it down and I leave feeling very useful. I have met so many people who respond similarly. Don't most of us have to face a decision at some moment: should I keep a list of self-pitying memories of injury, loss, disappointment, hurt, or can I move on to live my life in a more positive and generous spirit?

No one likes having dirty dishes in the sink for a month or finding dirty socks draped over a desk lamp (scene from a shared apartment). Or having hair all over the bathroom, or half-eaten slices of pizza, turning green, on the TV set, rugby sweatshirts full of dirt, blood, and sweat hanging in the shower. Living conditions may vary but many involve sharing space and facilities. Without mutual consideration, sharing such spaces leads to chaos, angry outbursts, and health hazards. Well, what's at stake in these situations is the good of others, the common good, and that is the rationale for the Holy Spirit's gifts. We hear in St. Paul: "To each individual the manifestation of the Spirit is given for the common good."

The Holy Spirit comes to form the nucleus of a new human race, one race of people who live for the good of the other and in peace.

Peace is the result of individuals like you and me, and nations too, being able to put the common good before petty needs, partisan politics, and special interests. "To each is given the manifestation of the Spirit for the common good" (1 Cor 12:7). We Westerners in our extreme individualism think, act, and vote so often in terms of me, my neighborhood, my wallet. The emphasis in Pentecost is on the Spirit giving a variety of gifts in order that we may use them to serve the whole body of Christ. The Holy Spirit is given to turn us "from isolation to community, from competition to cooperation."

How often we hear it said in praise of someone that so-and-so was or is so competitive, as if that were the crowning achievement of a human life! What about saying he or she always put the good of others ahead of his or her own? Or, that she or he understood that there is only one human race? Giving a sign of peace to those around us before Communion is a sign of our oneness with and goodwill toward not only these few people but with Somalis, Hispanics, Swedes, Iraqis, with men and women of whatever color, religion, social status, or income. Life in Christ and in the Holy Spirit means life for others.

One of the most rewarding aspects of people-watching is seeing wide-eyed, energetic little kids pulling their parents or guardians along the sidewalk or being pushed in a stroller or carried on the back. So often full of excitement, bouncing and utterly beautiful with their velvet skins, almond eyes, and little arms waving aimlessly. And in a big city they come in all colors and racial mixtures, providing an endlessly fascinating picture. It makes it all the more poignant and sickening to hear of tragedies involving children. The newspaper pictures a little Bosnian boy, blinded by a land mine, learning Braille. A friend asks prayers for his sister whose eleven-year-old hanged himself after a dispute with her about selling his saxophone to buy an electronic game. And to cap it all, the stories of children gunned down in schools and elsewhere—in Manchester, UK, Newtown, Connecticut. Or kidnapped: young girls in Nigeria.

All this, of course, is somewhat selective; we have become almost immune to continuing horrors in many parts of the world involving children. There doesn't seem to be too much danger of sentimentalizing children in our world. The uniqueness, beauty, and vulnerability of little children needs a lot more veneration. They are incomprehensible and inexhaustibly fascinating miracles not only for their parents but for all of us.

The large and popular downtown dining room is filled at noon with bustling men and women, many in their twenties and thirties, obviously at the beginning of their careers, eager and lively; there are older, more staid business types, too, and a sprinkling of tourists and shoppers. At a nearby table are a man and a woman, probably in their fifties, with a severely disabled person in a wheelchair who can barely be seen over the tabletop. The man goes to the buffet to get various items. The woman, a picture of gentleness and graciousness, sits with the person in the wheelchair. There are no signs of weariness as she brings the food to the mouth of the helpless one, only the most pleasant and smiling manner.

I don't know which does more to give one a broader perspective on life: the woman giving the care or the dependent person in the wheelchair. The grouchy clerk, the difficulty in finding a parking spot, the humid heat of the sidewalks, worry about work still to be done, even bigger matters like what the future holds, why so-and-so hasn't ever called, all these are cut down to size before such a scene.

Emotional overload some weeks. One year, for instance, graduation followed a week with the death of two first-year students in accidents, the suicide of the father of a senior, and the backdrop of a student's struggle with cancer. Graduation itself, for teachers, is a time of mixed and heavy emotions. One is often exhausted by the relentless routine of classes, class preparation, grading papers. To have the students leave is, in one sense, a relief. On the other hand, many of them have given us and others great joy, stimulation, and inspiration. For the graduates it is usually a moment of great exhilaration—combined with some sorrow at parting from many dear friends—and of looking forward to the "commencement" of a new life.

Most of life might be such a mixture of conflicting emotions and experiences. To simplify things and make them more manageable, do we sometimes just choose to ignore some elements? T. S. Eliot said that we can't really take too much reality at one time. Should we be more sensitive to all of it? Should we make more of a point of entering into all of it, even elements that contradict each other? Or should we concentrate on chosen elements and make the most of them? Is it true that at any one moment too much is always going on around us for us to absorb? Are we inevitably going to miss something important? Are we just too limited for the richness of reality? In view of that possibility, what do we make of our complaints about boredom? Where does boredom originate, outside us or from within? Do we perhaps not give enough of ourselves to the life around us? Enough questions!

"The widely held and unexamined notion is that death will be oblivion. We will be in total darkness, our bodies decomposing, our personality excised" (*Interview* magazine, January 1996). It's worth noting that the source of that remark, not a traditional Christian believer, refers to this denial of anything beyond this life as an "unexamined" notion. In reaction to too-easy comments about the beyond, many today believe that there is nothing to hope for beyond this life. Their assumption is that all that awaits us is oblivion, darkness, decomposition, and dissolution of personality; these are "unexamined" and unquestioned. Those who do the most questioning about afterlife are, it seems, the elderly for whom the prospect of death is more imminent. When young, following the latest rock group, our own future, the color of our hair, the football standings, and meeting the right person, we don't have time for death.

At a minimum, Christian belief that Jesus rose from the dead assures us that evil, sin, pain, death do not have the last word. There is new life for us. The unbelievers might have a point insofar as they seriously question the too-detailed descriptions about eternal life. Images drawn from a wedding or a banquet are the best we have and tell us something important while not giving us exact pictures. Weddings and banquets point to the sharing of love, between individuals and in community, and to joy and even excitement. Possibly all that frivolous stuff that fascinates us in our youth—no matter how long that lasts—is a good indication of what eternal life is. Why shouldn't a loving God tailor everlasting life to the God-given desires that propel human life and activity?

"Those who believe in God, but without passion in their hearts, without anguish of mind, without uncertainty, without doubt, without an element of despair even in their consolation, believe only in the God idea, not in God himself" (Miguel de Unamuno).[47]

That might seem a bit dramatic for some of us Northern believers but the point can still be taken. At some time in the course of our life of faith, there should be some questioning, some wrestling with what it means or does in our life. Whatever else that odd biblical story about Jacob wrestling with an angel might mean, it can stand for the need for some emotional, if not intellectual, struggle with what it means to believe in God, in Jesus Christ.

Most often this will be triggered by some shaking event: loss of our job, death of a loved one, a treacherous attack on our character, a persistent depression. Or, it might be occasioned by something less immediate and specific: boredom and/or apparently meaningless routine, continual failure, or disappointment in love. We only come to a compelling, personal vision of who God is when we let these situations shake up our belief, make us think, question, argue, even struggle with God. Not ever doing this leaves our relation to God on the same level as our relation to people with whom we have only a formal, nodding acquaintance. That would be believing "only in the God idea" rather than in the God who cares for us. We're better off complaining to God or questioning God in prayer, asking why, than keeping God at arm's length by not taking God's presence seriously enough.

"According to the ads, fresh breath and dry armpits are crucial" (line from the comic strip *Calvin and Hobbes*).[48] That line occurred in a dialogue about what is important in life. With possibly slight exaggeration, it points to elements in our culture that militate against the right priorities. One does get the impression from advertising that without the right mouthwash, Cindy will never give you the time of the day; that there is precious little that is more important than dry armpits and silky hair—and not in the same place!

It's not that most of us are going to take such ads with utmost seriousness, but the overall bombardment by them obscures what is important. Though it is usually not said explicitly, the same ads tell us by the type of models they use that well-tuned bodies and teeth with no unsightly gaps are absolutely necessary for a satisfying relationship. We all need, after all the gloss and glitter of the ordinary movie and television ads, to see and value people with inner qualities that only show themselves gradually but are vastly more satisfying and important than clear skin and straight teeth. It is refreshing but rare to see a movie where the hero or heroine has gap teeth, a weak chin, and a few extra pounds but human sensitivity and a genuine conscience. Without dropping our appreciation for beauty, we might value the more lasting qualities that make for good relationships and a happy life.

A few centuries ago our ancestors in Germany, Korea, Nigeria, or Poland would only have heard about the loss of a ship at sea months after the fact. If there was a famine in Ireland, the same thing. A tribal war resulting in many deaths in Afghanistan might never have come to their consciousness. Today within minutes we hear of the crash of a plane off Malaysia or of a terrorist bomb in Spain. Rapid communication makes it impossible to be unaware of the ever-occurring tragedies around the world.

You almost feel obliged to apologize for good spirits and happiness. Somehow you must make it obvious that you are aware of the suffering around you. It is not possible for us to live contentedly and simultaneously be oblivious to so much human suffering. What do we do? Do we continue to watch the news and get progressively more discouraged? Or do we refuse to read the news and live in a happier, make-believe world? As we prepare to enjoy the evening meal or go out to dinner, the TV is showing pictures of people being slaughtered in the Middle East or rioting for food in Somalia, women weeping for their husbands and sons taken away and shot. And all this on a small planet among people with the same feelings and hopes that we have.

One can justify a certain amount of depression in us well-off Westerners or first worlders. But, more helpfully, can we not do something by our votes and what we expect from our own country or the world? Can we not keep up some hope and good spirits so that we all don't despair or make everyone miserable? Active concern and sympathy are one thing; general discouragement and a sad face help no one.

"Remember," **Jesus says,** "where your treasure is, there your heart is also" (Matt 6:21). We are led to hard work, sacrifice, the expenditure of time and thought and means, even to suffering, by the strength of our devotion to someone or to some cause. What we are willing to work for and suffer for indicates what we regard as important, where our treasure is. Any one of us can test the strength of our devotion to God or anything else by asking ourselves: For what do we give up our own comfort and schedule? To what do we devote our time and thought, our best inventiveness?

What drives us, motivates us, even gets us out of bed in the morning? New parents know what gets them up from their sleep over and over again. Our Lord tells us that it is our treasure that draws us, what counts most for us, to which we give everything. It might be a bit uncomfortable questioning about this, but that is the direction of Jesus' teaching. "Where your treasure is, there your heart is also."

"There are three ways in which we may relate ourselves to the world—we may exploit it, we may enjoy it, we may accept it in awe" (Abraham Heschel).[49] By this time in human history, most of us first world people are familiar with criticism of our often selfish exploitation of the earth. I'd like to pass from that to the other parts of Heschel's statement. We might also, he says, enjoy the world and/or accept it with awe, reverence. To accept it with awe means, as I hope has been stressed enough here, to see every moment of life, every facet of our world, as a great wonder into which we've been placed. Something we are made aware of in times of death, tragedy, the arrival of love, the birth of a child.

Something, also, which we so easily forget. How about enjoying the world? Of the three this might be the most ambiguous. Exploiting the world sounds in general like an undesirable stance. Accepting it in awe sounds unreservedly good, appropriate. Enjoying it? That might suggest actually a kind of heedless luxuriating in it, using it in the throw-away fashion so typical of our culture. We see this in everything from litter to loveless sex. It can be a flip and irreverent draining of the good around us for our satisfaction. But enjoying the world can also be a way of expressing reverence and appreciation. Appreciating the good things of the earth, from melons to music, is a way of giving them respect and recognizing their value. We enjoy other people, certainly near the pinnacle of the good of this world, by treasuring and honoring with respect and love all that is admirable and lovable in them.

Relief workers speak of the difficulty of interesting well-off Westerners in the plight of inhabitants of dry parts of Africa, or the treatment of women and children in many spots, of migrants lacking all the amenities. Getting their/our attention is extremely difficult. They call it "famine fatigue." Through the capabilities of today's swift technology, people have been so bombarded with pictures of the starving, slaughtered, and suffering that they can no longer be shocked or even, possibly, feel compassion.

We could probably speak of "beggar fatigue" and "disaster fatigue" also. After passing in the course of the day fifteen to twenty people asking for handouts, we almost necessarily develop some protective shield. Is this another paradox of modern technology? The more swiftly and easily we can communicate, the more indifferent we become to others? The Christian must ask how we are to surmount this, what can we do to retain some sensitivity without being "fatigued"? Praying for others in distress is often denounced as a cop-out, a substitute for action. But in so many cases, there is little or nothing we can do at the moment. Why not at least retain some sensitivity by turning our sympathy and the wrenching we should feel into a prayer?

In the Old Testament Joseph, he of the "many colored dream coat," we see a vivid example of how changing circumstances can put a different face on the tragedies and pain of life. His brothers, envious of his favor in the eyes of their father, had sold him into slavery. Eventually he becomes a power in a foreign country, Egypt, and helps his family during a famine. He is even large-hearted enough to reassure his brothers, passing over their treachery. "It was really for the sake of saving lives that God sent me here ahead of you" (Gen 45:5). Joseph is able to see in his position in the Egyptian court an opportunity. He would never have become the Grand Vizier but for being sold into slavery.

The good that can come out of awful events is at the heart of our faith. We have it put before us when we commemorate the suffering, death, and resurrection of the Lord at Mass. Out of evil God brings triumph and joy. We might have become accustomed to looking at the minor trials of life this way. We see how missing that long-awaited trip was providential in that we were able to be with Mother when she became ill. We might even be able to see how being laid up with a broken leg taught us some compassion. How far can we go with this? Certainly, it's safer to learn something ourselves from such misfortunes than to urge the same lessons on others. We hear frequently how some local tragedy, say the death of a teenager in an accident, brought together the whole neighborhood. A great good, in a sense, came out of a terrible tragedy. We are safest in praying that we ourselves learn from the example of Christ how life can come out of sorrow and even out of death.

As I write, my spot in this city is on the border between the financial district and the very popular Chinatown. What a difference a block makes! Morning, noon, and early evening in the financial district you walk through very earnest, purposeful crowds. People move fast in their businesslike dress toward a goal, even if it's only lunch. Certainly and fortunately, many do have time for civility and friendly conversation, but they don't just dawdle. A block away the tourists stroll and saunter through Chinatown with no schedule to follow, no place they have to be, joking, talking, gawking, oohing and ahhing at this or that sight.

People on vacation are at their most relaxed, carefree, enjoying each other's company, with time for a cappuccino, a cold beer, or an ice cream, forgetful of all their healthy eating habits. Being on vacation is a bit like dancing, enjoying music, water sports; we live at those times without an immediate purpose, enjoying the present. The fact that we punctuate our ordinary workaday life with things like dancing and music underlines the need we have for such breaks from a driven life. Vacations are more extended examples of the same. Paradoxically, we make it our "purpose" at times to introduce more "purposeless" moments into our life. Otherwise we risk passing through life never having actually enjoyed it for itself. "Look at the birds of the air, the flowers of the field. They do not sow or reap, yet your heavenly Father . . ." (Luke 12:22-31).

Deferred gratification might be a term for the way I regard letters. Going to the mailbox and finding a personal letter, one hand written (!) or at least printed, is a great delight. I'm caught between tearing it open and reading it as I walk to my room or office or saving it till I can sit down and enjoy it undistracted by anything else. Even a postcard from a friend in Bangkok or Calgary qualifies.

So often, too often, everything we do is done with something else as background: we write or study with music or even the TV; we drive a car while eating breakfast or talking on the phone (please God, none of these!); we lunch while discussing the fate of the world or, more likely, our business. We are not used to giving what is before us our undivided attention. This seems heightened now with acquaintances passing you by absorbed in something else on their smartphone. We exchange a greeting in church while looking over the shoulder of this stranger to see if there's someone there we know. All this is a pretty shabby way of treating what is supposedly our prime concern at the moment.

Taking a letter and sitting down comfortably to read it (a good cup of coffee might go well with it) is a great pleasure. I think there's a lot to be said for making this experience available to our friends by writing them real letters, what the contemporary devotees of high tech call "snail mail." If we can never "find time" to do this, could it be that we are letting human matters, human relations, others' need for us, take the back seat to a lot of less-than-human preoccupations? The people we love deserve the attention we can give them.

Thomas, unlike some of the other apostles, is mentioned in all four Gospels and described in more detail in John. From the latter, we get our warrant for referring to a Doubting Thomas. The account of Thomas's doubts is well known (John 20:24-29). Preachers over the centuries have pointed to Thomas as an example and encouragement for our faith. We see in him someone who clearly was not gullible but yet believed in the Lord. Many others have aided our faith in one way or another. The faith of any one of us rises on the foundation laid by many others. None of us receives faith simply on our own, much as we like to credit ourselves.

Thomas and many others have contributed to our faith: parents (obviously), friends, teachers, pastors, the Gospel writers, other authors, even critics of faith. Thomas may have believed, as Jesus says, "because you saw me." But most of the rest of us have not seen but have learned to believe because of the words and examples of others. Our faith is part of a broad and long connection to the faith of many others. Faith illustrates something which is true of so much else in life: we are what we are, we have our belief, our hopes and trust in God because of and through others. How much, too, we depend upon the support and example of each other. We have not seen, we have not touched the Lord but, impressed by others, we have believed.

Worship, Mass, sacraments are meant to celebrate the presence of God's power, help, grace. They should make more evident at this moment what we theoretically know is always true: God is present, near, loves us, is with us. Yet the actual experience of Sunday worship can be anything but helpful. The sound system works fitfully; there is a continual disturbance near us; the music depresses us rather than lifts us up; the preacher sounds lifeless, unprepared, or irrelevant. And all of these can happen at one service! We leave feeling we have been involved in a losing battle for some encouragement and nourishment. What do we do? Go home resentful and angry? That just makes it worse. This particular Sunday might be the exception, the coming together of all the worst possibilities.

Perhaps there's something we ourselves can do about all this, something we can offer. Possibly we should look into finding a Sunday worship that is more helpful to us. To go back Sunday after Sunday for more frustration and a depressing experience might be too much. If it's simply the exception, we probably should realize that our attendance was something we "offer up," a service where we offer God our disappointment rather than our joy. One sees parents with little children who every week come and spend a very distracted hour torn between what is going on at the altar and walking little children. They must offer God their good intention and be contented with that. Possibly such people learn more about sacrifice than those for whom everything goes smoothly.

In Buddhism the ideal person is enlightened or awakened. He or she really sees things as they are. The man called Buddha who lived five or six centuries before Christ would be more properly called "the" Buddha since the word means the enlightened or awakened one. On a basic level we'd all do much better if we were awakened, alert. So much of our life we live like half-awake beings, zombies, unaware spectators, inert witnesses, or transients just sitting by the road. We're like the stereotypical fellow sitting under the awning of a small town store on a hot, lifeless afternoon, if not totally asleep, at least half snoozing.

Throughout life we're often awakened momentarily by a death, some tragedy, a momentous event in the family or among friends. We're awake for a while but soon go back to sleep, back to our more or less unconscious state, going through life like robots. Our life is often like the way we listen to a Scripture reading in church: before we know it, the reading is over and we have no idea of what was read. Instead of being in charge, we're like fall leaves blown about by the wind, at the mercy of whatever is happening around us, at the most responding rather than initiating.

How unlike the psalmist who says in two different psalms: "My heart is ready; my heart is ready. I will awake the dawn." Usually we're fortunate if the dawn wakes us up; the eager psalmist speaks poetically of awakening the dawn himself. Can't we somehow prolong those periods when we are awakened and alert, alive, so that more and more of life is that way? So that the unconscious moments become fewer and fewer? So that we value and cherish the people and opportunities around us?

We haven't read yet of three- or four-month-old infants organizing to oppose dependence on their parents. They aren't conscious of their need for a diaper change or for food as some lessening of their freedom. Only as teenagers are they really offended by their dependence on adults. And in popular culture dependence is often understood as a sick relationship, a lack of personal control, an inability to stand on one's own two feet. This goes so far that, for many, dependence has no simply neutral meaning but is always a bad thing. Possibly only time and experience teach us about legitimate dependence, teach us that we have not made ourselves, that we do not live simply on our own in splendid isolation. We "depend" on others for our shoes, our medicine, our food, for breathable air.

Even our "dependence" on God for our existence is resented by some. How would they react to Jesus' words: "Apart from me you can do nothing"? Or, in the same context, "I am the vine, you are the branches. He who lives in me and I in him, will produce abundantly, for apart from me you can do nothing" (John 15:1-8). Clearly, Jesus is not talking about our ability to tie our shoes or operate a computer. He is stressing that the strength we need to better our world, to begin each day with hope and courage, to persevere in the good, all this is made possible by our sharing in his life. Our dependence on Christ does not limit us but allows us to do what our weakness and lethargy would not. If we live in him, we live with his strength.

The rugged individualist ideal persists. We meet it in real life and in fiction and movies. We meet it in others or in ourselves. Whether it is stated so baldly or not, this ideal (the word *ideal* is generous) implies that we made ourselves and every feature of our personality; we can stand by ourselves and are not affected by others. It's hard to see how one could take all of this seriously and some of it is possibly a pose.

The rugged loner pose inevitably falls short. For instance, say we are surrounded (or seem to be) by grumpy old men, grumpy old women, grumpy old kids even. No matter how hopeful we are, how enthusiastic about life or someone or our work or our travel, the presence of this bunch tends to pull us down. We cannot simply live amid cynics, complainers, bitter and unhappy people, pessimists, the non-responsive and not feel the oppressive atmosphere. The number of crabby people per square foot definitely affects any one of us. Conceivably there is someone of heroic mold who can live amid this day after day and still be positive and hopeful. Most of us, even if we don't take on the cynicism or anger, at least are weighed down by it, find our smiles harder to produce.

What we can do is make an effort to bring the opposite spirit into our environment: our hope, faith, and accompanying joy; our trust in God and the essential goodness of others; our conviction that a negative spirit helps no one. We are affected by the grumps around us, and others depend on our good and positive spirit to counter such influence.

We are made in such a way that we must use words even to say how limited they are! If we wish to point out how inadequate is our language about God, we have to use words. I will use words here to emphasize the importance of silence, of the absence of words! We have an inkling of the significance of silence in the experience of friends who feel so comfortable with each other that they don't have to think of things to say. Silence shuts off the noise that really prevents us from hearing our own selves and God. Talk and noise are a barrage that makes sure no other messages get through. Think of how so many public places have to have noise or some kind of sound going all the time to make sure no one, God forbid, starts to think! Or feel! Or pray! Often noise masks our fear of facing ourselves or any serious thought about life, its direction, our actions, our end.

Too, words restrict us to the kind of thinking that can be expressed through words. More profound thinking or feeling often is just too subtle for the clunky character of words. Lao-Tzu is credited with this: "Those who know don't talk. Those who talk don't know."[50] We come back to the paradox we began with: we are such social beings that the thoughts and feelings that well up in silence often call out for expression. People turn to everything from poetry (straining at the limits of words) to music to dance to bring out what seems ready to burst from within. Aldous Huxley wrote: "After silence, that which comes nearest to expressing the inexpressible is music."⁵¹ Some of us break into song at times especially of joy and well-being in general. Not such a bad idea . . .

"What a friend we have in Jesus." (My unchurched father in his old age and nearly deaf could be surprised at times alone in his house singing "what a pal we have in Jesus," a variation probably more due to failing memory than a desire to be hip.) Just hearing that line from an old-time hymn might strike some Christians as too chummy or simply undignified. Churchgoing people get so used to the formal language of the service that "what a friend we have in Jesus" seems a bit like proclaiming sweet-nothings to a date in a public auditorium. Yet Scripture itself warrants the language of friendship. In John 15, Jesus talks about laying down his life for his friends: "You are my friends if you do what I command you. I no longer speak of you as slaves. Instead, I call you friends, since I have made known to you all that I heard from my Father."

Revealing ourselves to another, opening our hearts to another, is the sure sign of friendship, a necessary step in fostering it. In turn Christians have every right to turn to Jesus in times of great need or turmoil. Moments of exhilarating joy or crushing sadness drive us to open up to a friend for comfort and understanding. Similarly, why shouldn't we open ourselves to the Lord in such times? In any budding relationship we encourage intimacy by a willingness to open up, to risk self-revelation. Jesus says he has made known to us all that the Father has told him. We have every reason to think: "What a friend we have in Jesus." Or, as St. Benedict writes in his Rule to his followers: "Let them prefer nothing whatever to Christ, and may he bring us all together to everlasting life" (RB 72.11-12).

How mixed, how unsure, how confused our thoughts and feelings can be! When, if ever, do we really understand ourselves and what we really feel or think? We say one thing and live and act as if something else were how we truly felt. To be organized consistently around a core of beliefs that all hang together might be ideal, but who achieves it?

I thought this difficulty was well illustrated in this story: In advance of a visit to alumni of the college in a particular town, Ed from the alumni office called former students living in Hillsdale. Rather gruffly, Al Burnside said over the phone: "I hated all of my four years at Bildad College." Ed speaks a bit more with him and before the conversation ends, Al says: "If you're going to be coming up here, bring me a few loaves of that bread they make there."

Possibly we could say his head says I hated the place while his heart (the stomach?) has fond memories of it. Mercifully, even our hate and dislike are not total; even an unpleasant experience might have had its tolerable moments. We talk about sorting out our feelings and that seems a good term for what we often need to do. What do I truly feel or believe or think? Some introspection, some time, the different perspective that comes with distance and age, all might help us figure out who we are and what we think. We need patience with our own inconsistencies as much as we do with those of others.

There was a song quite a few years ago entitled "The Tender Trap" and it was about marriage. Calling marriage a trap might seem a bit flippant, but we can take it to mean that marriage draws two people into the kind of self-giving and sacrifice we would otherwise never imagine. If we don't like the word *trap*, we could say that marriage seduces us into these things, attracts us with the promise of love and intimacy into a life that entails, we might say, almost more than we bargained for.

With the arrival of children, couples find they must inevitably give up much of their freedom, time, and comfort to take care of dependent little beings. They have no choice about getting up at two in the morning to have a sick child vomit on them even though they might have serious responsibilities the coming day. Parenting means giving, like the poor widow whom Jesus commended in the Gospel (Mark 12:38-44), of what we might seem almost to lack: time and energy.

Parents are often not giving of their surplus of energy and time; they are already, as we say, "run ragged." The widow, and parents, remind us all that true giving, true sacrifice, is not of what we have left over, but of what we could use for our comfort or convenience if we didn't give it. Statistics on giving to charitable causes show that the poor widows still give the most: people of lower income give more proportionately than do the wealthy. As we recall the Lord's self-giving, we ask to be strengthened in our own willingness to give.

People asked to choose a New Testament text for some occasion very often come up with the Beatitudes, the first part of the Sermon on the Mount in Matthew's Gospel: "How blest are the poor in spirit. . . . Blest, too, are the sorrowing, the lowly . . ." etc. (Matt 5:1-12). Yet, where do we begin talking about or understanding them? One way is to note how the ideals given there by Jesus are in such contrast to those of our society. How different the values in the Sermon on the Mount are from those featured in the heroes of *People* magazine or the *Wall Street Journal* or in a health and fitness magazine. There, good looks, material success, aggressive take-overs, lavish lifestyles, and earthly fulfillment are preeminent.

What Jesus says God blesses are attitudes and conditions we would just as soon think of as little as possible. Sure, the newspapers or the TV news will highlight occasionally a person of extraordinary selflessness or heroism or even suffering. But generally, we only reluctantly think of these things. Fulfillment for our society has to come within the span of our earthly lives. We are to be pitied if we don't have a cushy retirement or reach our potential in a well-paying, powerful position. Jesus puts forcefully before us the fact that our fulfillment, our happiness might be deferred but is most sure for those who suffer, sorrow, are persecuted, are merciful, are generous, who are peacemakers.

To speak or not to speak. To express all our feelings or to hold back. To let it all hang out or to maintain some reserve. As happens so often, we do well to mistrust a too-simple decision in favor of one or the other. "For everything there is a season. . . . A time to keep silence, and a time to speak" (Eccl 3:1-7). Possibly only a life anchored in prayer and closeness to God will enable us to make the right decision at a particular moment.

In words that reflect so well the over-simplified prescriptions of contemporary culture, Elizabeth Wurtzel has written: We've been taught "that if people would just say how they felt, a lot of problems could be solved." She goes on: "I come from a family where no one ever hesitates to vent whatever petty grievances she might have, and it's like living in a war zone."[52] Clearly, the writer feels that some things might have been better left unsaid.

Though it will not solve all the complexities that surround speech and silence, the words of the Epistle of James are worth reflection. He says the tongue is "a restless evil" and that no one can tame it: "We use it to say 'Praised be the Lord and Father'; then use it to curse men, though they are made in the likeness of God. Blessing and curse come out of the same mouth" (3:8-10). To speak or not to speak?

We know of various saviors and religious teachers whose teachings have survived, in fact flourished, for many centuries in various parts of the world. In Acts 5, the Jewish teacher Gamaliel tells his fellow Jews, upset about the teaching of Jesus, that if these teachings are from God, there is nothing they can do to prevent them from flourishing. The teachings of the Buddha, of Mohammed, of the Bhagavad Gita have all flourished and continue to influence new generations.

Therefore? In our time, after centuries of a much narrower attitude, the Catholic Church in its weightiest pronouncements (those of Vatican II) went on from this to say that it "rejects nothing of what is true and holy in these religions." Further, these religions "often reflect a ray of that truth which enlightens all men and women."[53]

"Catholic" with a lowercase "c" means universal, all-embracing. How refreshing and expansive if we were to rediscover more of this generous self-understanding in the word *Catholic*. How did Catholic ever come to mean restrictive and narrow as it does for some? Our faith in Jesus Christ, if rooted deeply in prayer and reflection on Scripture, does not require a hostile attitude toward other religions. Rather it should give us the self-confidence to see them, to study them and use the elements they contain of insight into God, the meaning of human existence and how to live.

A psychiatrist back in San Francisco from a sabbatical working in Zimbabwe says: "I've resumed my work here. Let me tell you, work is highly overrated. The pace here is hundreds of times faster than it was in Zimbabwe. We miss it and suffer from ongoing culture shock. There are aspects of American culture to which one should never become accustomed."

This amounts to a graphic way of pointing out that we need to have some slow time, some silence, some place for reflection in our lives. In the lives of some of us, lives lived daily in high-tech areas, there is probably very little space even for the kind of talk we read here. The utilitarian, the bottom-line, the immediate monopolizing of every minute. Some even take it home with them.

In such a fast-paced existence, there is not even time to dwell for a moment or two on how others feel; everyone is presumed to be a sort of flesh-and-blood machine with emphasis on the machine. In big cities that, thank goodness, seem to have more and more wooded or grassy spots, it is encouraging to see people on their lunch break at times lying on the grass watching the clouds or sitting with arms back simply looking. There are ways in which we can find or make space for our spirits in our lives. Often, I suspect, it would even have the effect of bettering things within our families too. We all owe it to our own selves, our humanity, to find, to take some time to reflect, to wonder, to muse, even to dream.

"Although the fig-tree does not burgeon, the vines bear no fruit, the olive-crop fails, the orchards yield no food, the fold is bereft of its flock and there are no cattle in the stalls, yet I will exult in the Lord and rejoice in the God of my deliverance" (Hab 3:17-19). Profound faith or infinite deception? Is the writer expressing an incredibly pure faith in God, one free of all this-worldly assurances, or is he an example of believing at any cost and despite every bit of counter evidence? We believers will tend to see this as evidence of great trust. Skeptics will say that this is typical of what faith means: believing despite the lack of evidence. As Mark Twain said: "Faith is believing what you know ain't so."

The last words of Habakkuk do hint at something he has to go on. He speaks of the "God of my deliverance." Possibly something in the past justifies his trust; God has come through in some crisis. Most believers would be likely to have some such assurance. There are, however, many much more desperate situations where, like Habakkuk, we hang on to our belief in the midst of what seems to be signs of God's absence and indifference—in times of abandonment by friends and family, times of incurable disease, times of devastating sorrow. A mature faith (which is fundamentally a great trust) persists in trusting God in whatever happens because of strong convictions that God is finally concerned and does truly love us, and happy experiences in our life justify that faith.

Both the content and the manner in which it is given bother us or even offend. Jesus says in the Sermon on the Mount, among many other equally disturbing things: "You must be made perfect as your heavenly Father is perfect" (Matt 5:48). The manner: a command! The content: to be perfect!

We have a hard time picturing ourselves as perfect; we're so aware of our irritability, self-seeking, wrong desires, rash judgments. In the context of earlier words about loving not just friends but enemies, what Jesus is saying makes a bit more sense. He has asked that we be like the rain and sun, which do not distinguish among human beings. Our love, too, should be all-embracing, extending way beyond the people we naturally like or who are close to us.

This is a bit more specific than being perfect like God is perfect, though it certainly isn't any easier! Our love and goodwill are so easily drawn by certain kinds of people, by such externals as their appearance, their smiles, their personalities, and, let's admit it, their class and customs, their manners. Jesus asks us to do so much more than that: to love the unlovely, the unattractive, the downright painful, the irritating, the uncongenial, the ones who don't seem to care a bit about us. We would be doing well if we simply tried today and then the day after and so on to show some genuine kindness to someone for whom we have no natural attraction. By such little steps we work toward this steep ideal of loving everyone.

The Gulf War brought a lot of wrong—if not false—prophets out of the woodwork. They packed people in to churches and laid out a scenario where the Gulf War was the opening phase in the final battle between good and evil, Christians and the Antichrist. No matter what the political situation might be, the turn of the century, the year 2000, brought out a crowd of would-be seers announcing the end. Joined to the year 2000, earthquakes, wars, pestilence, the ever-present impression that everything is going downhill, these will inspire people with no more knowledge than you or me to tell the rest of us that this is the end. They claim special access to the mind of God. Jesus says: "Be on your guard against false prophets, who come to you in sheep's clothing but underneath are wolves on the prowl. You will know them by their deeds" (Matt 7:15).

The early Christians wrestled with the problem and decided that if the so-called prophet asked for money or anything for oneself, then he or she was suspect. But even that is not as simple as it sounds. There is so much room for self-deception, on the part of the speaker or the hearers. The more one thinks about it, the more it seems clear that no single individual has the key; discussion by many members of the Christian community and attention to the full voice of tradition are required. The safest course for all of us is not to jump too eagerly on the bandwagon of some person claiming special messages from God or Mary. Along with that we are right to expect any authentic message to lead to more love, more attention to Jesus and his words, more service of others.

Those who read the Scriptures much or hear them often are aware of what divergent pictures they give of God. In some passages of the Hebrew Scriptures, God seems fiercely judgmental and threatens severe punishment. Elsewhere we read of a God who cares for people like a mother. Many different faces of God emerge from any survey of the centuries of writing involved in the Bible. Any one image of God, if it alone is in our minds, limits God too much. There is a God who judges; there are limits to what human behavior God tolerates; and there is a God pictured in Jesus and spoken about by him who wishes to console and calm the storms of life. Familiarity with diverse pictures of God might save us from packaging God in too slick a manner.

God is always more than we can imagine; God is always more, for instance, than some kind of a servant at our beck and call. As Jesus teaches by resting placidly in the boat during a storm (Matt 8:23-27), we are right to call on God and to trust God. But, as the Our Father teaches, our petitions need to always be accompanied by our recognition that God's way of doing things is different than ours; God's plans might be other than what we would like. Our faith and trust need to reach a point where we feel free to trust God without spelling out exactly what God must do.

Bumper stickers, T-shirts, and pickup trucks sport the words: "No fear." It seems to be an expression of youthful confidence and daring. Once we're past our twenties, it becomes more difficult to brag about our freedom from fear. Worries, cares, and responsibilities pile up; the laughter is less spontaneous; the whole approach more cautious. Some of that might be inevitable but let's not believe that too easily. One of the qualities of our faith should be a genuine and deep confidence and trust in the Lord, a trust that casts out at least some if not most of our fear. Our Lord, after telling his disciples of all the tough consequences they might face, encourages them: "Do not fear those who deprive the body of life but cannot destroy the soul." He even says: "Do not let them intimidate you" (Matt 10:24-33).

He goes on and stresses God's care for us by saying the hairs of our head are numbered. And once again: "So do not be afraid of anything." How far we are from this total trust when we let ourselves be oppressed with worries and cares. How difficult it is to entirely surrender ourselves into the loving care of God. We generally would rather keep control ourselves even if it means a worried, harassed existence. Lord, give new life, even youth to our faith, our trust, our confidence. Francis, the first ever Jesuit in his position, certainly does his best to give new life and youth to our faith.

Another mass killing, this time in a theater; the homilist at Mass describes it as "perverse grandiosity." He says we can—we must —still value "the imperfect beauty of this impossible thing called life" and deliver what bits of healing we can. If we take our eyes and thoughts off the horror, we find much in ordinary daily life that is kind, thoughtful, generous, even tender.

A few minute examples just recently in my own life and observation; within the space of two hours I experienced much of this. At the restaurant where I had gone for dinner, the friendly bartender omits the glass of wine from the check. I begin to point it out and he shushes me: "I know what you're going to say. Just shut up and enjoy it." I thank him. As I board public transportation, a man immediately opposite the door I enter gets up and gives me his seat (I do sport a cane; and such consideration on big city public transportation is almost invariable). As I prepare for the always chancy exit from the crowded bus, a man standing next to my seat moves away and offers me a couple of encouraging smiles and I exit fairly easily. As I exit another bus to which I had transferred, the driver apologizes with a smile for letting me off a foot or two from the curb. An elderly woman struggles to bring her purchases to the cashier who greets her: "Good afternoon, young lady." A young man escorting his woman friend takes the time to offer his arm to an old man about to clear the curb and walk across the street.

Healing, of course, thank goodness, is all around us on a much larger scale: in the ministrations of medical people; the tender care given elderly parents; the time and attention given to little children by family members; the sympathetic ear offered by friends, counselors, teachers; the volunteers at the soup kitchen or in Uzbekistan. All is not "perverse grandiosity." Nor is it ever really trivial. Such gestures are simply homely and good but not negligible. Sensitive healing and availability to others recognize that what we do for the least of our fellow travelers on this planet is done to Christ.

The dissolution of the Soviet Empire and the liberation of Eastern European states from its control brought great joy and relief to many people. Such great empires, their leaders, and their values are most often opposite to the approach of Jesus. While the great empires may be able to make the trains run on time, they bring no one genuine happiness. Even their leaders realize little from gaining the whole world by force; in the process they destroy themselves. Neither you nor I, of course, is going to offer much competition to Alexander the Great, to Napoleon, or to Stalin but on our own level we can be at times persuaded that power-plays, ingenious strategies, cunning, and self-seeking are the obvious ways to happiness and fulfillment.

Jesus teaches a paradox which sounds like nonsense to the world of politics and power seeking. "If you lose your life for my sake you will find it" (Matt 16:25). By surrendering to the power and life of God in us we attain, better yet, are given a fulfillment we ourselves could never have devised. Salvation and fulfillment are, in the Bible and Christian tradition, not something we attain from a series of seminars or some guru. It is a gift of God to those who surrender, open themselves in poverty of spirit to allow God to work in them. "If you lose your life you will find it."

"Stay awake. You cannot know the day your Lord is coming" (Matt 24:42). Most of us could use some reminders, like those in Lent, to live attentively, not to be forgetful of the end of things. What is more difficult for us than to stay awake and to be alert? Throughout our lives we have these alarms in the form of accidents, illnesses, deaths of people close to us, yet find ourselves forgetting the impact they made at the moment. It's not simply the elderly who find it hard to stay awake past eight in the evening; it's the young, too, who in other ways so often live half-consciously, oblivious of opportunity, wasting time.

To be more alert, more attentive, is so important that some religions, like forms of Buddhism, sum everything up in mindfulness. It's immensely productive of genuine living. St. Augustine, great theologian of the Western tradition, probes his own spirit in his famous autobiography, *Confessions.* In a well-known passage he remarks on how even though God was present within him, he was so often absent. God is present and close to all of us; life and its possibilities are available to all of us. We either meet them alert and wakeful, or we are oblivious of the passing moments. "Stay awake. You cannot know the day your Lord is coming."

To reason or not to reason, that is the question. Or, less poetically but more accurately, what is the place of reason in our lives? Most of us would give it some place. We all say things like: "Be reasonable." Or, "Why did you do that?" Or, "What are your reasons for suggesting that?" We get suspicious of people who seem to leave reason out of everything. We complain that he or she acts on whims, apparently with no thought. But there are limits to reason! "Reason," Pascal writes, "is really a poor thing if it cannot recognize its own limits." Our craftiness has to be corrected at times by what looks like the unreasonableness or foolishness of God's ways. Our reason, after all, is only human.

The cross of Christ is certainly a complete challenge to reason: God overcomes sin and death, it tells us, by allowing the Son to be put to death. It makes no human sense. When Peter lowered his nets into the water at the Lord's command after an unsuccessful night of fishing, it wasn't reasonable (Luke 5:1-11). He knew that the night was the best time for fishing. But he puts his trust in One who is above and beyond human reason. The lesson for us is not to let reason put limitations on what God can do in answer to faith and trust. Every time we pray in difficult or desperate situations, we affirm that God is not limited by what our reason says is possible. "Reason is really a poor thing if it cannot recognize its own limits."

From the writings of St. Paul it's clear that the first Christians celebrated the Eucharist, the Lord's Supper, in the course of a daily meal. The Jewish predecessor of our Eucharist, the Passover Meal, was (and still is) celebrated in the context of a meal. Eventually it became necessary to separate the Eucharist from a regular dinner because some had too much good food, which embarrassed poorer members, and others drank too much. Such disparities pointed more to division than to the unity celebrated in the Lord's Supper. Coming together at the altar should strengthen our unity, bringing us into union not only with God through Christ, but with each other in the body of Christ.

All our tendencies to judge others harshly, to envy, even to wish others failure, to consider them for whatever reason inferior to ourselves, all of these that we might bring to the Eucharist are opposed to its meaning. Hence, we begin the Lord's Supper asking forgiveness for our sins. Every time we come, we are beginning again in the constant struggle to live up to the unifying love of a genuine Christian. The unity of the Eucharist is not some lockstep uniformity but a willingness to respect and honor others who might differ from us on many matters but agree with us in finding the meaning of life in Christ.

Before we come together for Communion we again remind ourselves that our unity with God has to be accompanied by goodwill toward others. We do this by exchanging the sign of peace. And immediately before we receive the bread and wine, we take on our own lips the words of the centurion: "Lord, I am not worthy to have you enter my house. Just give the order and I will be cured" (Luke 7:1-10).

"I think of the college so often. I look at the poverty which surrounds me here (in Central America) and realize how truly lucky I am to have had the opportunity to attend a private college. So many are never given the same chance." The writer was a First Lieutenant on an army exercise in Central America. What an eye-opener such an experience is for a young man from a comfortable Midwestern suburb, the graduate of a small liberal arts college.

The old saying "*Noblesse oblige*" comes to mind. Security or position, privilege, give rise to obligations. Many another young man or woman in a similar position in any number of countries of the world has experienced the same sense of the privileged life they have had. The point of talking about it is not to regret or denigrate the comfortable life of these people but to be happy that the new experience makes them more aware of privilege and its responsibilities. And secondly, to hope that enough of this will affect the way we affluent people live and act and vote.

Waiting an hour or two in the airport, I tell myself and have told myself often that I should do some reading, make good use of this time. And I do have a book with me. I find it hard to do the reading. No, the noise doesn't bother me and the lighting is satisfactory. The human pageant, the human parade, is too endlessly interesting to take my eyes off it and limit them to the written page. They go by in such variety. I'll never be able to see all of them. Just in itself the variety is seemingly unending. They're young and old, healthy and infirm, sauntering and almost running, smiling and grim, in every color of complexion, every height and diameter, dressed in high fashion or extremely informally, long-haired or short, on and on.

I argue a bit with myself: should I make a deliberate effort to read or let myself be amazed by the new faces and figures that go by? The latter usually wins. We take trips to see the Tetons or the marvels of ancient Rome or the pyramids. I might enjoy that, but I think watching the human race go by is equally worthwhile. In 1 John, we hear the writer argue that if we do not love the people we see, how can we love the God we do not see? The point is that if we cannot find something lovable in the visible creation, how could we love an invisible God?

The well-done celebration of Sunday Mass can be, even in some rather incidental ways, a reminder about otherwise neglected aspects of ordinary human life. The effort and dignity the woman puts into proclaiming the first reading; the beauty and richness of the baritone voice leading the singing; the time spent in greeting others and wishing them peace; the reverences made to the book of the Scriptures and to the altar; the individual attention in the distribution of Communion—all these speak of the value and dignity of human beings, of human life, of all the visible as well as invisible elements of human life.

One is reminded for an hour or so at least that the earth and our fellow human beings are valuable in themselves apart from the opportunities for gain, for advancement, apart from what they can do for us. One comes away from such a service refreshed, one's youthful excitement and delight in creation restored. The general and easily banal affirmation of God's love for the earth and humankind becomes something genuine and specific, referring to each human being there. Besides affirming the place of God in our lives, worship can celebrate the goodness and worth of every element and person in God's creation. At the center of it all is our remembering that "God so loved the world that he sent his only-begotten son into the world to save it" (1 John 4:9-10).

Weekday Mass in most parishes is pretty low-keyed and predictable. While there might be some music, the general tone is rather quiet and contemplative. Very often the same people are there day after day. In a big city one inevitably has the experience of that familiarity being disrupted some time or other by the entrance of a homeless person, a disoriented or mentally troubled street person. He comes in and talks to the nearest person somewhat unintelligibly, kneels, sits or stands, usually at other times than the regulars. Those nearby will try to be calming. Whether one sees such people on the streets or in the more unusual setting of weekday Mass, they seem—they are, of course—so out of place.

The streets on a weekday are full of people busily moving about on errands connected with commerce, with making money. The street people, the homeless, or simply those who do not, will not, fit into ordinary society suggest for one thing that we do not give persons enough time and attention in our world. One can't help thinking how their lives might have been different if someone was able to pay more attention, to give more time. The fact of God's love for every human being has to be made real here and now by some Tom, Dick, or Mary. The people who drift in and out of our world with apparently no anchor are reminders of the great value there is in loving attention to another human being.

The very upbeat hymn caught my attention—"We Build a New Tomorrow"—as I looked on Sunday morning TV while away from home. It was a broadcast of the Sunday morning service of a very well-known preacher, accused at times of pollyanna-ism. And the production is certainly very slick, smooth, and clean. But, granted all that with whatever negative overtone that brings, the service is encouraging, inspiring.

I can see how it would be a welcome bit of refreshment for the crowd of people who are there, who have gone through five or six days of drudgery and worry, battling traffic and dealing with testy people, doing repetitive and boring work, unhappy over a failed relationship. Such an encouraging and lively service would only be wrong, I think, if it meant we simply and completely ignore the seamier and sadder side of reality. Just to face that—and it is either in us or around us, for sure—requires the strength of hope and joy. For Christians that should come primarily and ultimately from the light of the world, our refuge, our strength, our hope: Christ the Lord.

Patience: I see a lot of what it entails as I, a house guest, watch Ned and Jill getting Sally and Tim ready for school and themselves ready for work at 6:30 a.m. Tim will not eat, except maybe to pick the raisins out of his cereal; Sally goes to the table but cries rather than eats. Sally would like to milk her recent cold for another day of missing school. Jill and Ned work on the kids, cajoling this one, exhibiting infinite patience looking for the missing shoe. What an education the children have been for these two and for many others like them. And for the observer. The parents learn somehow to manage all this and still get themselves off to the job in a positive state of mind.

Did the feisty and impetuous Ned and Jill I might have met in a college class ever expect to develop such patience and inventiveness? Life, work, unanticipated situations, and turns in our course all teach us things we would never have learned otherwise. If only we could see all these as opportunities rather than simply painful interruptions of our normal schedule and way of acting. Possibly it's too big an expectation but I think we can all manage at least at times to accept more gracefully matters that try our patience with the belief that some good will come of this.

An eleventh-century Benedictine monk born in Italy, St. Anselm, lived a life that doesn't seem too unlike the mobile lives of our times. He became a member of a monastery in France where he had gone to be near his mother's family after a quarrel with his father in Italy. Eventually, he became archbishop of Canterbury in England but that didn't end his travels. In that position, disputes with the English kings over control of the church led to several exiles. All this without benefit of air travel, automobiles, or railroads. He managed, too, without a laptop to write a number of books on theology and philosophy, which continue to influence theology today. Not only his mobility but his thought has relevance for millennial people.

One famous line of his is even helpful to mortals like you and me: "I believe in order to understand." Those of us with some inclination to rationality would more easily comprehend a saying like: "I understand, I investigate, in order to believe." And for many there is much truth in that. We study, question, think, in order to strengthen our decision to believe in God and Jesus Christ. Anselm's line, "I believe in order to understand," stresses another, less obvious point. Not only should some thinking precede faith, but faith should provoke more thinking, give us more understanding. Faith is not a way of ending all questioning but of opening up new questions and broadening our understanding. We who use our minds to understand economics, tax forms, golf, computers, how to program a new smartphone, can certainly use them to unfold the meaning of faith, of what we believe.

In Tobit 13 the author, speaking of Jerusalem, the holy city, voices the hope that "within you the Lord may comfort every exile, and within you God may love all those who are distressed for all generations to come." In Scripture, Jerusalem is often a picture or foreshadowing of what the church should be. Many images of the church could profitably be replaced with the one given here: a place where the exiled, the distressed in any way, the suffering and oppressed, the poor and ignored would find care and compassion. Wouldn't that be a lot better seeing it as a "field hospital" (words of Pope Francis) than seeing it as another large corporation, bureaucracy, or power structure?

Despite all the theoretical definitions that are given for the church, in reality it becomes what we, its members, make it to be or allow it to become. We still have a way to go in overcoming the definition, given by someone in the nineteenth century, of the church as an organization of bishops and priests to which laypeople may belong. The quotation above suggests an attractive vision of the church as the place where the love and forgiveness of Jesus are continued and shown in flesh-and-blood individuals. Francis echoes this: "The Church must be a place of mercy, freely given, where everyone can feel welcomed, loved, forgiven and encouraged to live the good life of the gospel."[54]

Novelist Jon Hassler admitted that dialogue he heard in restaurants and other public places was suggestive and helpful for writing his books. I was struck late one Saturday morning at the remarks I overheard while walking in a part of the city clearly very popular with the young and trendy. For instance, two young men on the street talking as they walked past me. Number one says: "She left you?" The other says: "Well . . ." That's all I hear but the last remark suggests that her departure was a bit more complicated.

While lunching a bit later, I hear a woman say to a friend: "I'm two years from forty." Clearly a bit of concern there about aging. A bit later I hear two others in their late twenties, I'd guess, talking as they go by. Number one says: "He's antsy." The other asks: "About what?" Number one: "The rent."

The area I'm in and all the beautiful young people around hint that a certain appearance and address might push people to live a bit beyond their resources. The topics in these snatches of randomly heard conversations are of universal interest. One touches love, friendship, intimacy. Another, our inevitable concern about aging. And the last, the unavoidable economics of daily life. Love, growing old, money. How much more basic can you get? These are the same matters we should unhesitatingly bring before God in our own unique words of prayer. Like the fellow walking alongside us on the street, God is a good listener and even more.

Conceivably there are some exceptional individuals, perhaps only inexperienced and too protected, who feel that encouragement is unnecessary. But most of us need it daily. And, fortunately, we often get it from husband or wife, family, friends. That can all change, of course, with the loss of one of these stalwart supports in our life. "Encourage one another while it is still 'today,'" Hebrews says (3:12-13). It's unlikely that any one of us will ever feel that we've had too much encouragement. (It's close to love and compliments; do we ever get enough?)

God encourages us through the example of others; through their words, gestures, calls, visits, letters; their taking the time to gauge our feelings. And, more wordlessly, through their example of love, faith, confidence, even joy. Keeping a high and even cheerful confidence in the Lord is helped by like-minded friends, fellow parishioners, associates. God knows there are enough sad people in our world who do not have this confidence. Showing this confidence and joy ourselves is a gift we can give the world.

Wouldn't it be great to be able to call into work "grouchy" (as well as sick) and have that honored; to hear the supervisor say, "Sure, we wouldn't want you around if you aren't feeling your usual cheerful self." Or, better yet, we'd like to hear that the continual grouch we work with would call in "grouchy" and stay home. (In fact, usually it's the others who are grouchy, isn't it?) Should we wear our bile on our sleeve today? Do we have to share our bad moods and ill temper with the rest of the world?

Unfortunately, most of us don't have the option of calling in grouchy and remaining in solitude till it passes. We have meetings scheduled, tasks to do, people to meet. It would be great if we could somehow forget the bad mood or temper; if we could convince ourselves that brooding over some ill will not help, that we should set it aside and go on with living. This is one place where the civilities of ordinary life combined with an effort to be more concerned about others might help. Really, why should we feel that we can inflict our sour spirit on others? Why should the rest of the world feel as bad as we do? Could respect for others lessen our grouchiness, lighten our heavy mood?

There's more than one way to imitate the saints. I was encouraged to hear that during one of her stays in the hospital, Mother Teresa had called her community to tell them she would be home the next day. The papers reported that her doctors disagreed. During my few hospital stays, I've always felt in a very short time that I was ready to leave only to have the doctor disagree. Possibly the lesson is that no patient is patient enough to like staying in a hospital. (Before it became a neutral term for a resident in a hospital, the word *patient* derived from a Latin word meaning to suffer. Maybe the two meanings are irretrievably linked.)

To see such a holy woman share my impatience is really encouraging! It's always good to realize there are respectable people who are as impatient as you are. Or it might be that any active person, forcibly confined to a bed or prevented from activity, feels the same frustration. Even to have satisfying work curtailed by the flu is maddening to a person who finds satisfaction in his or her work. Some might find the confinement and limitations on activity a blessing. Bravo for them. The rest of us have a patron in Mother Teresa.

"Life always ends before it's finished" (Walter Ong, SJ). I'm guessing the only people who would not say that are some elderly who are hanging on in pain, isolation, and loneliness. When we're still caught up in our work, our families, friends, and a variety of interests, there never seems to be time enough. We want to finish the house, the summer cottage, see the grandchildren, get to Italy. We look inside and there, too, are faced with unfinished matters: the temper still flares up; we're still too quick to judge; a deepened prayer life has been put off yet another year.

How do we interpret the fact that a glorious smile or an attractive person can still make us melt? It scares a seventy-year-old to think that he or she is still capable of infatuation. Should we be over that in our later decades or should we take that as a sign of vitality and sanity? Our intentions still seem an odd combination of self-seeking and self-forgetfulness. Where's this integrity or wholeness they always talk about? The incompleteness of everything might be frustrating. On the other hand, it might be a strong pointer to the fact that this life is not meant to be complete, an encouragement to hope for more beyond it. The theologian Reinhold Niebuhr said: "Nothing worth doing is completed in our lifetime; therefore, we must be saved by hope."[55]

People in the time of Christ and the apostles thought in terms of a smaller world and a shorter history than we now do. The early Christians expected that the end of things would happen in their lifetime. Paul tells his readers not to be too concerned about getting married if they aren't (1 Cor 7:25-31); the time is so short it is hardly worth getting the license. Today, we are aware of the vast distances in our universe and its immense age. The universe and time might seem endless but human life seldom gets much beyond a hundred years. Our tears, our rejoicing, our purchases, our building, our pleasures, our ambitions—they are all ultimately passing. We need not despise these things or consider them of no account. No.

Our grief and joy, even our home and choice of work, are extremely important. But somehow we must also be able to see beyond them. This is what Paul means in the same passage when he writes: "Those who weep should live as though they were not weeping, and those who rejoice as though they were not rejoicing. . . ." He tells us that these, too, shall pass. Our lasting treasure is deeper and survives the tears and joy; it's found in God and our relation to God. Christians cannot regard this world and its contents as so important that they will do anything to get what they desire. Perhaps we have to admit that we're at a disadvantage compared to those who have no belief in anything but the world they can buy, touch, and collect. Christians believe we are also citizens of a world that cannot be bought, collected, or touched, but which lasts forever.

Dusan from Bosnia, speaker at a luncheon honoring entrepreneurs, was asked about failures in his upward trajectory. He said: "Of course, there were some." But, he added: "Failure in the evening; an opportunity in the morning." In a broader context there is a line from Psalm 30:6, "At night come tears, but dawn brings joy." This is verified in the experience of many. The pains and worries of the day often do dissolve with sunrise. I emphasize experience and often because this is not a philosophical or theological truth or a magic formula though it is related, of course, to trust in the here-and-now effects of our Lord's death and resurrection.

Many of us have gone to bed at night in the course of our work and responsibilities or more personal concerns, bothered by some issue that seems irresolvable. At times the problem may be too personal even to be discussed with family, friends, or fellow workers. It could be some difficulty about a schedule into which a wrench has been thrown. Or concern about what seems to be the stubbornness of another party regarding some issue. It could be a worrying accusation. Or what seems to be an impossible demand regarding a piece of work.

I think Psalm 30 echoes what so often happens when we pray about the concern, leave it up to God, and then roll over to sleep. (Ha, I know; not that easy!) This isn't a formula—above all, it isn't magic—but what seems to be so often the experience of many of us. In the morning we find the accusation was all a misunderstanding; our worry had been cut down to size; or the other party has relented about the use of that space. The problem has disappeared like the morning fog. This is "old hat" to the more seasoned, the tried and tested, but possibly a viable suggestion for beginners in what is called the "real world."

The forty-year-old father was concerned about teaching his sixteen-year-old daughter to drive. In the process, he had to combine some guidance with a willingness to let her really take over the wheel, to take charge. Too much direction would defeat the whole process; too little, of course, could result in an accident. "I have to let go and bite my tongue at the same time." In many ways the process of teaching a child to drive a car is a good picture of the whole changing relation of parent and child or of anyone who has to introduce another into a situation where she takes over eventually.

The teacher has to figure out when to say something, when to make a correction, when to refrain from saying anything. It must surely be one of the most difficult and worrisome features of being a parent. God has gone to extremes in this regard. God has made the universe and its creatures, allowed all their powers to develop, and then seems willing to sit back and let us take charge. We can use our intelligence to save the world, to cure diseases, to feed the hungry. But we can also use our powers to grab all we can of the world for ourselves or to destroy it. All this suggests that we reflect about how we use the freedom, the ability, the opportunities we have while respecting and treating tenderly the same in others. How are we using our control of the wheel?

The return of students to school in the fall, at least as I know it, to a residential college, is for many, both students and professors, an exciting time. Add to it the more energetic and crisp fall weather in this part of the world and you have a vibrant mix. Students are so happy to see each other, to get away from an often tedious summer job (mowing lawns, cleaning up at a nursing home, folding boxes, or in some other way competing with robots); some are even excited by the prospect of new classes, new material to study and think about. And there is, of course, the resumption of athletics—the football season, for instance.

But the happiness and excitement of even these privileged young people has its down side. One student was burnt over his whole face and body, hospitalized for nine days injecting morphine into himself in order to tolerate the pain with two months spent in recovery; another, at twenty, has chronic back problems requiring continual treatment; another speaks of having to move out of the house along with his mother and siblings to get away from an abusive father, of restraining orders and an impending divorce. Others have broken up a relationship and are still smarting from that; even though that may pass, at the time it is often dangerously crushing. The carefree days of college ("the best years of your life," the older always tell students) are often also punctuated with tragedy and agony. All the more reason to cherish now the joys and excitement.

The Irish writer Oscar Wilde complained to a fellow author that the latter's new book had offended him endlessly. Why? Because the author hadn't mentioned Oscar. To varying degrees, we are all similarly self-absorbed. As far as we're concerned, there is nothing important except what concerns me and my preoccupations. More forgivably one gets this impression from couples getting married; on that day nothing else really is happening in the universe.

But there is a kind of self-absorption that we should resist. It shows itself when we are totally unable to think of others, to be aware of their needs or preferences. Instead our own moods must be put on display for everyone to enjoy; after all, we think at such times, what else matters but the fact that I'm in a foul mood or even a very exuberant one? Why shouldn't the rest of the world take its cue from me? It seems so obvious. Such an attitude is something we probably all go through at some time or other; it seems to be characteristic of many of us in our more unpleasant adolescent moods.

The example and the power of Christ in Scripture and Eucharist are meant to help us reduce this self-centeredness, to be able to think of others, even to place their interests and needs before mine. Obviously, this is what married people must do for each other; what parents do for little children. In his Rule, St. Benedict includes under "The Good Zeal of Monks" the steep admonition: "No one is to pursue what he judges better for himself, but instead, what he judges better for someone else" (RB 72.7). Christ assures us that making a habit of this dying to self leads us paradoxically to a richer and deeper life. Losing, forgetting myself, is the way to finding my better self.

College students, especially those away from home for the first time, have some wake-up calls. New situations prompt an internal audit: "Oh, oh, I will have to do the laundry!" "Dad won't be prodding me to get up." "To drink or not or how much to drink . . ." Profs and staff will provide other wake-up calls. Of course, life now or later brings even more serious ones to all of us.

Recently a speaker of some fame and popularity did just this as he spoke to more than a million young people. He warned against a very dangerous kind of paralysis that could easily plague any of us: "To think that in order to be happy all we need is a good sofa. A sofa that makes us feel comfortable, calm, safe . . . A sofa that promises us hours of comfort so we can escape to the world of video games and spend hours in front of the computer screen. It is very sad to pass through life without leaving a mark. But when we opt for ease and convenience, for confusing happiness with consumption, then we end up paying a high price indeed: we lose our freedom.

"It pains me to meet young people who seem to have opted for 'early retirement'. I worry when I see young people who have 'thrown in the towel' before the game has even begun or who are defeated even before they begin to play, who walk around glumly as if life has no meaning. Deep down, young people like this are bored . . . and boring! But it is also hard, and troubling, to see young people who waste their lives looking for thrills or a feeling of being alive by taking dark paths and in the end having to pay for it."

These wake-up calls are courtesy of Francis (aka, the Pope) on World Youth Day, July 30, 2016, in Krakow, Poland!

As I walk by the student mailboxes one morning, a student has just pulled a postcard from his box and lets out a loud and happy yell. After looking at it, he calls me over and shares with me the card from Dave, a mutual acquaintance, who has been spending a semester in Sweden. This fellow, busy with school and many other activities, is thrilled, excited by a postcard from a friend. This isn't the only excitement in his life. There's classes, friends, football, parties, working out, hanging out, music . . .

I was reminded of a phone conversation with a woman in her eighties who had moved into a new senior citizens' apartment complex recently. After lunch, she said, they sit in the lobby and wait for the mail. These people aren't playing football or preparing for an, as yet, undecided future. They don't enjoy a lot of social life. They live for a visit from an old friend, a phone call from a daughter, a note from a son or grandchild. It takes so little from you or me to cheer the life of one of these. What do we lack? Time? Will?

There is something unique about a letter or a personal card that has advantages over a phone call, e-mail, or even a perfunctory visit. A letter can be opened again and enjoyed, can stimulate thoughts and memories. The process of writing it required some thought and putting down a bit more carefully than what we might say to someone face-to-face. For believers, letters are one of the most tangible assurances we can receive that God loves us, that we are loved.

"In your prayer do not rattle on like the pagans. They think they will win a hearing by the sheer multiplication of words. Do not imitate them. Your Father knows what you need before you ask him." Jesus introduces the Our Father this way in Matthew's Gospel (6:7-8). Prayer has to consist in some listening as well as in words. We act in prayer at times like a person sitting nervously with a new acquaintance. We feel we have to be saying something every minute; we find little pauses embarrassing. How different it is with someone we know well. We can sit together, listening to music or driving without feeling that one of us has to be saying something every second.

Prayer seems often to lack a bit of space, some silence, some room for God to influence us or get a word in. True prayer has to be a dialogue. God's work in us requires that we leave God some opening, a chance to influence us, a chance to be heard. In our world of so much noise and so little tolerance for silence, it might be hard for us to learn to be quiet before God, but take a phrase from Scripture and keep coming back to that gently while trying to concentrate our attention. Silence and attentiveness can be learned.

American writer H. L. Mencken often gave us more sparks than profound enlightenment—though he's fun to read. In a preface to one of his books he wrote that as he got older, he thought it too bad that we only have one life to live. His thought was that the human being should have at least two: "One for observing and studying the world, and the other for formulating and settling down his conclusions about it. Forced, as he [any human being] is by the present irrational arrangement, to undertake the second function before he has made any substantial progress with the first, he limps along like an athlete only half trained."[56]

We can all recognize how ill prepared we often feel for life, no matter our age. From the Lord's teaching we have the guidelines; theoretically we know what we should do. But we are still impatient with matters which we long ago thought we had accepted. Snap judgments still come all too easily. In quiet moments we think we understand how we should react to disdain but in the actual moment, that's all forgotten. We understand that patience and gentleness are the right way, yet . . . we are always still learning—or at least being taught.

The Christian recognition that we are all inevitably flawed and will remain that way, that we need God's continual help and forgiveness—this is something we can bring to supplement Mencken's vision. Yes, theoretically, we never have enough time to observe and understand our life; yes, it might be helpful if we had another lifetime in which to practice the following of Christ and his way of living. . . . But all that relies too much on mere human ingenuity, intellect, will, etc. Our fumbling and stumbling are really constant invitations to leave a bit more, a lot more, up to God.

Criticizing a song, "Welcome to the Real World," a reviewer writes that for the composer, "bumper-sticker platitudes like 'God is love' still soften the blows of the 'real' world." For the critic, "God is love" is a tired, meaningless phrase repeated by lazy people, about as significant as "This vehicle makes wide turns." That's one reviewer's reaction to a phrase that antedates bumpers by at least 2,000 years. The implication is that a more original or striking phrase, whether true or not, would be better.

But does the phrase "God is love" soften the blows of the real world? In the context above, it's clear that to soften the blows is to refuse to face what really is. The reviewer's point itself, however, qualifies as a platitude: that religious belief is a way of fooling ourselves in the face of an unfriendly universe. War seems a constant in human history; and so are murder, oppression, hatred, victimization, abuse. We can, of course, balance that by citing all the love, generosity, simple goodness, even heroism that exist.

In the critic's mind is the assumption that goodness and love cannot be real. That would be "wish-fulfillment." Somehow what we desire and long for—love, peace, goodness—is excluded beforehand. Why? The reviewer believes that our deepest desires are doomed to frustration, that God cannot be love. We can say more. The people who try to deal with the world's woes are often those who do believe that "God is love," that love has been given us in Christ, and that we must share it. Welcome to the real world— where hate and bad things coexist with love and good deeds, where we know both terrorists and firefighters.

Inevitably for a Christian at all reflective about her or his own life there comes the realization that through some pain, some suffering, some agony of my life, I know what it means to share the cross of Christ. It might be through something the Lord did not go through like cancer or the loss of family members in an accident. Or it might be through something very much like his suffering: being misunderstood, persecuted, falsely accused, harassed by someone or some group. Psalms that complain of enemies out to destroy the psalmist become painfully comprehensible, no longer references to some remote and unimaginable situation.

The first kind of suffering, from disease or catastrophe, leaves us pretty innocent. The other type, more like Christ's, might, on closer analysis, be more like the crucified thief's crucifixion. As he says to the other one crucified with Jesus, "We actually deserve some punishment; this man has done nothing" (Luke 23:41).

If we have earned the enmity and opposition of others, there might easily be some flaw in us that precipitated it—that, at least partially, accounts for it. The fact that our cross might be somewhat self-induced only adds to the anguish and pain. Villains and good guys are not clearly distinguished. Identifying with the cross might mean, among many other things, simply accepting more of the ambiguity and messiness of human life. The villain and the hero both live within us.

A friend, a young father (let's call him Rog), takes care of three children most days while his wife, their mother, works as a physician. The children benefit from an energetic and high-spirited dad who almost matches their energy. Part of their education at the hands of dad is visiting regularly the elderly in a nearby home, particularly one Amelia. Amelia has been bedridden for a long time and on this particular day the staff say she seems comatose, but Rog and the kids are welcome to stop in. They go in and make an effort to speak to her but with no response. She indeed seems comatose. Finally, they decide to leave and as they approach the door, they hear a hoarse voice from the bed say, "Thank you for coming."

The cross is everywhere today. We see it on walls and in paintings, of course, hanging in churches and homes but also from the ears and necks of rock stars. We see it so often that it loses its impact. In Christianity we celebrate it, too, at every Eucharist and in special feasts and seasons. It's also present more concretely, even emotionally, in the ills and pains of human life. John says in his Gospel that Jesus had to be lifted up on the cross "that all who believe may have eternal life in him" (3:13-14). Not simply that we will have eternal life but we may have it now. Eternal life begins now; it is not only for the world to come. It shows itself in healing, renewal of our spirit, in hope and joy. The cross of Christ saves us from death and also helps us now.

If we take the time in our next sorrow, bad mood, disappointment, discouragement, anxiety, bitterness even, to look at the Lord on the cross, we can find it says a lot to us. It tells us, whether we are crushed by our own sorrow or that of others, that God's own son has shared human sorrow. Not only has he shared it, he is still with us in every pain and danger, assuring us that through the cross we come finally to victory and joy. The cross tells us that the poor, the suffering, the homeless and ill, the abandoned have a brother, a fellow sufferer in the Lord. In a most special way, the Lord is with us and we are close to him when we must suffer or undergo any of the difficulties and pains we call the cross. Our sharing in the remembrance of the Lord's passion at his supper goes on outside the church building in the unavoidable pains of daily life. So that we have even now eternal life.

I was going to write that any significant event in our lives has both joyful and painful aspects but, on second thought, leave out the significant. On third thought, all that seems too great a generalization. There are moments—a walk in the woods on a beautiful fall day, a musical performance that completely sweeps me off my feet, a good dinner with congenial people—when everything seems perfect for the moment, when no pain mars the occasion. In the other direction, maybe the same thing: lying in bed with pain pounding away in the joints, we are totally miserable, feeling completely out of synch and out of sympathy with the situation to the point of tears.

But so often, pain or joy which seems to be in control is possible only because we forget for a moment the opposite: The people who are enjoying time in the hot tub under a starlit sky are content because, for the moment, the difficulties with the fifteen-year-old have been put aside, the painful situation at the office is forgotten, as is the disappointing outcome of the basketball game earlier in the evening.

Our work might be really satisfying, something that challenges and rewards, but it, too, has aspects that are simply irritating. We can probably see the value of enjoying those great moments untroubled by the thought of pain elsewhere in our lives. But how do we face the primarily stressful and even agonizing moments? Is perspective the key? Reminding ourselves that this is only part of my life, only one of the experiences of an otherwise happy life?

> In some things all, in all things none are crossed,
> Few all they need, but none have all they wish;
> Unmeddled joys here to no man befall,
> Who least hath some, who most hath never all.
> (Robert Southwell)[57]

The hope of Christians is a good shared by Christians of all denominations, something that sets us apart from those who have no hope. This hope is in Christ and the good he promises, even beyond this life; it is not something to hug to ourselves but to offer the world. If it is to convince others, it has to be more than just a private comfort. It must inspire us to work for the betterment of human life, for good here and now, for the oppressed and poor, the victims of injustice and neglect. Those who have no hope might be inclined to say, "Why bother? Nothing is going to change."

We fail in hope when we ourselves believe and act as if nothing we do could ever be of any use and that we must wait for the Lord to intervene. Waiting for the Lord to do everything might sound like hope, but genuine Christian hope spurs us to concern for the world. Since hope is not the same thing as optimism, even those who have a more melancholic nature can have it. It doesn't mean ignoring reality, ignoring suffering, but seeing through it to the Lord's love and care for the world. Hebrews says: "God will not forget your work and the love you have shown him by your service to his holy people. Our desire is that each of you show the same zeal till the end, fully assured of that for which you hope" (6:10).

We fear promises. A man in his twenties says apropos of his generation: "My generation, we cohabit for six to eight years, get bored, and move on. We are afraid of marriage." Promises do cut off other possibilities but only so that we can give ourselves unstintingly to this person, this place, this purpose. Promises are commitments that free us from endless floundering and indecision. We go from superficial wine-tasting or grazing to the real banquet of life. We give ourselves to this person or this undertaking and stop looking over our shoulder to see if there is something else we'd rather do, somewhere else we'd rather be, someone else we'd rather love. No one is suggesting, God forbid, that a college sophomore has to decide now on a career or life's companion. Edison checked out hundreds of filaments before settling on the right one for his lightbulb.

Commitment means that after a decent search, we do choose engineering over teaching or Bill Schwarz over Nate Olson. That we quit looking for some impossible blend of Taylor Swift and Mother Teresa. Often our outrageous expectations of others only mask our own unwillingness to change. We need practice for the big commitments. It means beginning with manageable promises: to stay with an exercise regime three times a week or with prayer every evening, to produce what is promised on time, to take out the trash. Our commitments reflect God's untiring love for us and are fueled by it. "The steadfast love of the Lord never ceases, it is new every morning" (Lam 3:22-23). The love of he who loved even to death on a cross makes it possible for us to be faithful to commitment.

A letter writer in a popular magazine wrote that church attendance was dwindling because the message in church was not relevant. Ordinary people are primarily concerned about getting home safely and not being mugged on city streets, he said; people should be told in church not to do such hurtful things. One must have serious doubts that those who do drive-by shootings or mug pedestrians are at Sunday services waiting to be told that these things are wrong. I think we have to look elsewhere for the causes of crime than lack of preaching about it to churchgoers. And, similarly, dwindling church attendance must have another explanation. What churches and church services are primarily for is worship, prayer, praise, thanksgiving. The church shouldn't quit her mission of worshiping God in favor of moralizing to "the choir" about crime.

Our hope lies in getting more people to see the relevance of worship and prayer. Someone has put it: "The right relation between prayer and worship, on the one hand, and conduct is not that conduct is supremely important and prayer might help it, but that prayer and worship are supremely important and conduct demonstrates them" (William Temple). Worship implies that the solution to violence and outrage is not in moralizing but in building women and men imbued with love and respect who in turn build a world of love and respect. We have love and respect for others because we know that we are loved by God.

So often as adolescents we come to the conviction that we would be so much better off if we could get away from this oppressive family and religion and live our own life, a free life. We feel we must strike out, find our own way, even if it looks mistaken to our family. Undoubtedly, some experiment, some breaking of the bonds is necessary and those of us who are on the parent end of the affair need patience and great understanding. Part of it is our need as we mature to find ourselves, assert our independence. As we might know all too painfully, this leaving home can be anything from civil and orderly to brutal and disruptive. How hard it is to see those we love seemingly turn their backs on us and all we value.

The revolt of our children or our revolt against our parents is often a messy and unpleasant business. Parents, as in one lesson of the famous Parable of the Prodigal Son in Luke 15, have to keep the doors open, allow for the resumption of communication. The son or daughter might not see any need for that—at the moment. But a welcoming, forgiving parent is often needed when the prodigal discovers that there are, after all, some genuine values at home. Most of us have the rich opportunity at some time or other in our lives of playing from the heart the forgiving, welcoming mother or father. We have been forgiven much; it was always on condition that we would forgive too.

One can see that persons of integrity and character don't run for public office. They know that once you do, you become a constant target for attack; your private life is over. Even the slightest lapses become fodder for the press and other politicians. Think of what an unforgiving press or public could do with the Old Testament heroine Susanna. She was falsely accused of adultery and vindicated by the prophet Daniel (Dan 13:41-62). Then there's the woman taken in adultery in John's Gospel (8:1-11). She was apparently accurately accused but forgiven by Jesus. The case of Susanna would be spread over the media for days before being resolved; the vindication would be in small print weeks later. But, as is almost always true of Scripture, don't these two women stand for us?

Like the woman taken in adultery, most of us have failures in our past, if not our present. Like Susanna we are open to accusations, false or true. Our only security is in God, conscience, and the faithfulness of friends. If, despite failures in the past, we are trying to live a good life today, we need to trust in our own intentions and God's acceptance. Further, we all contribute to the climate of our society by the severity with which we judge. Do we impose outrageously unrealistic standards on others while excusing ourselves? From daily and frequent contact with Christ in sacrament and prayer we might learn some of his forgiveness and understanding.

"The elusive Higgs boson is at last found—and the universe gets a little less mysterious" (*Time Magazine*).[58] We are intent on getting rid of mystery. Science, of course, must probe both the macro and the micro. But even though astrophysicists delve deeper and deeper into this amazing universe, we cannot but be struck by how each new discovery opens up new depths. In popular language, we are justified in saying how mysterious it is. Even the birth of a child, despite what we know about the science of it all, still seems mysterious enough to us that we say: "What a miracle!" And we've all heard: "Why she ever married that guy is a mystery." In our thinking about difficult subjects, mystery can mean giving up prematurely on reason. The hard-pressed teacher, badgered by some precocious little dear, may finally have to say: "It's a mystery." But the word *mystery* has a much more profound sense. It refers to the unfathomable depths of reality, both human and (for lack of a better word) non-human.

While wiping out mystery may be a legitimate goal and part of the process in science, in religion doesn't it seem more questionable? Doesn't it ignore the complexity of human relations and decisions? Religious leaders too easily bow to our desire for clarity and certainty. In doing so they deny the ambiguity and multifaceted character of reality. If we reflect at all, we should resist too much clarity regarding messy human situations and the awesome reality of God. Thank goodness, Pope Francis is not among those who have all the answers free of mystery and messiness. He recognizes the ambiguity and depth of human life. For instance, "It is reductive simply to consider whether or not an individual's actions correspond to a general law or rule, because that is not enough to discern and ensure full fidelity to God in the concrete life of the human being."[59]

To overcome death summarizes perhaps most completely the deepest hopes of the human heart. So much of life is spent in overcoming lesser deaths: illness, disappointments, heartbreaks, and bereavements. The church uses the words of the Psalms to express the joy of Christ and of us in him: "You will not leave my soul among the dead, nor let your beloved know decay" (Ps 16:10). We celebrate the realization of these great hopes in Christ—and through him, for all. We are drawn by the Scripture texts to breathe deeply of the joy and hope that is ours in the Risen Christ.

Year after year we can hope and expect that our sense of ultimate overcoming of sin, suffering, and death will grow, become more deeply rooted. It is God's gift and comes to us to the degree that we put our trust in God's power over all life's hardships and pains. Making our own the words of the psalmist can help strengthen this hope and joy. "Since you are at my right hand, I shall stand firm. And so my heart rejoices, my soul is glad; even my body shall rest in safety. You will show me the path of life, the fullness of joy in your presence" (Ps 16:8-11). Alleluia!

To visit the sick or elderly once in a while is certainly good; that's evident from the way it rejuvenates the person who is laid up or unable to get out. To volunteer to help out at a food shelf or a shelter for the homeless is good. To take one's turn driving the neighborhood kids to a game is good. To stop in at a church and pray one day is good. To make a few days' retreat at a religious center can definitely be energizing. To do any good act one time or for a short while is probably better than never doing anything of the sort. But it's not quite the same as persevering in one of these practices over the long run.

Visiting an elderly family member once is not the same as being there day in and day out for that person, experiencing her good and bad times, her joys and sorrows. It doesn't make the same demands on me as a regular habit would. We can come away from several days of prayer and religious routine quite enthusiastic. But that doesn't give us the sense of monotony and sameness that the regulars experience. The real test of any good thing we do is perseverance. Otherwise it's just another bit of variety that punctuates our life. To continue a practice when it becomes dull and wearing is something different from the excitement of doing something the first time. To persist in a good practice "in sickness and in health, in good times and in bad" proves the genuineness of our "virtue."

Praying is rarely easy for us; we can use occasional reminders of what it should be. St. Therese of the Child Jesus wrote that she found prayer books full of beautiful but unusable prayers and the Rosary almost impossible to pray. Her advice was that prayer should be simple, direct, in our own language without worry about eloquence or grammar. It is, she said, "a lifting of the heart, a simple gaze turned towards heaven, a cry of thanksgiving and love in the midst of trials or joy." There are many other ways of saying it but this is worth reflection. This stresses the basic simplicity of prayer, something one easily forgets when reading detailed works on the subject.

Lifting the heart or gazing toward heaven is a wordless matter, a matter of simply turning our attention from present concerns to God; we don't have to use words with God any more than we have to go beyond a simple look with some close friend who understands us.

The second part of her statement gets to words—or at least sounds: a cry of thanksgiving or love. In some situations it could be no more than a groan that life provokes, one of those sighs—or, let's hope, maybe a whoop of joy, a "wow." We needn't worry about God being puzzled. Any words we use are more for our benefit than God's. We need to express them. God knows them. Therese says we should do this in trials or joy; that should cover most of life. We may, however, need to prod ourselves to pray in joy; so often prayer is thought of only as an interior 911 call. But why not speak to God, too, when we are bursting with joy, enthusiasm, excitement, happiness?

Cancer, war, accidental death, addiction, abuse—all these are more likely to be our enemies than an enemy lying in wait with a gun, though in our violent world we can't rule that out either. When we first read the psalmist, for example, in Psalm 143, "Lord, listen to my prayer. . . . The enemy pursues my soul," we might wonder how it could apply to us. More frequently, our enemies are those listed in the first line and even more internal ones like laziness, avarice, discouragement, indifference. But the prayer of the psalmist fits these beautifully too: "The enemy has made me dwell in darkness . . . my spirit fails; my heart is numb within me." How like the feelings of a person suddenly hit with a diagnosis of very serious cancer.

Our difficulty leads us to share the psalmist's sentiments: "I remember the days that are past." How good they were; how happy I was, how healthy. The twists and changes of life are so incomprehensible, so hard to figure out. Why is this happening now? Will I ever be able to really laugh again? "In the morning let me know your love for I put my trust in you." Make things different tomorrow—or soon. "Rescue me, Lord, from my enemies," from this disease, this crushing disappointment. "I have fled to you for refuge. For your name's sake, Lord, save my life; in your justice save my soul from distress. . . . In the morning let me know your love for I put my trust in you."

Choice vacations, good clothes, good looks, health and fame, at least money—all these seem to impress most of us to some degree. And that's true even if we know that they don't necessarily tell us anything significant about a person. If we do get more to the interior of another, it is often to be impressed by their intelligence or superior education, intellectual gifts. We're still not at the heart of a person, the character; that is often recognized only with difficulty and more slowly, if we can get beyond all the less important qualities.

For a man like St. Francis, so free from the influence of all the externals, even education was a dubious undertaking. As he saw his followers increase, he was distressed to hear that one group in Bologna, Italy, was planning a school. We would certainly regard a school as a desirable enterprise. But for Francis it suggested a departure from his primary concern with the inner life, the following of Christ; and it signaled, for him, the possibility of putting too much emphasis on what the world values.

The challenge for all of us who prize the good things of our world and of human life is to realize they are all of less importance than the heart, than our relation to God, our character. Often we only come to this appreciation by experiencing the shallow attraction of the externals, by seeing how little they mean.

In a large room crowded with several hundred happy and excited alumni milling around before brunch—after all, they're seeing old friends—it's a bit unusual to find oneself with a fifty-year-old successful businessman in tears. Everyone else seems to be talking about the football game or recalling crazy events from years ago. It's actually hard to carry on the conversation, he is so full of tears. My amazement shows and he says: "I've just come from a visit to the cemetery. Seeing the graves of so many of my old profs and friends (brothers and priests who taught in the college) . . ." More tears.

It's touching to see his feelings about the death of these people and, too, I suspect, really about the relentless passage of time. In the midst of so much enjoyment of the present, of friends, the mellow fall weather, blue skies and brilliant trees, mortality is a poignant thought. No matter how strong our belief in resurrection, new life beyond the grave, it's hard, at least in health and the prime of life, to accept an end to all this. While we're on the way to accepting—if we ever do—the fleeting character of all we prize, we could do a lot worse than shed some tears over it.

Jude and Kay are rather ambitious newlyweds whose first "job" has been volunteering at a food shelf and homeless shelter. They say one thing that struck them was how close we all are to the situation of the people using the food shelf. As one of their clients said: "Many people would be here with us if they missed a few paychecks." Though we all do our best to secure future paychecks by doing good work, there are factors present over which we have no control that could leave us without income. The economy, changes in demand for goods or services, restructuring of a corporation—these are all forces beyond our control.

It's not that way in our life as Christians. There is no arbitrary force, certainly not God, that is going to do us in. One still hears occasionally that one can live a good life, be serious about the following of Christ, and still somehow fall moments before death into some heinous sin that will cut us off from God. That might make for sensational drama but it's not consistent with human psychology and the way God works. We are only judged in terms of our conscience and our freedom. Even if the latter is limited in some ways, Christian belief about salvation presumes that we have enough of it to say Yes or No to God, to good, to evil.

Again, that Bishop of Rome (Francis) refreshes and inspires. Recalling his time as a superior in the Society of Jesus, he says: "I did not always do the necessary consultation. And this was not a good thing. My style of government . . . had many faults . . . I made my decisions abruptly and by myself . . . My authoritarian and quick manner of making decisions led me to have serious problems . . ."[60]

A humble leader of the church gives us two helpful examples, whether for our lives as parents or in any capacity where we manage others. Obviously, unlike the usual style of people with such great authority, he admits faults. He says he acted too abruptly and with too little consultation. This should sound familiar if we have any self-knowledge and even if we haven't explicitly ever admitted the same fault. Admitting mistakes is humbling, good for our spirits, and inspiring to others.

And the content of the fault is instructive. How often, theoretically to save time or to be more efficient, have we decided that we know enough, or we know it all? In the process hurting others, possibly demeaning them, and leaving those affected less receptive and possibly even hostile. Enough said . . .

I find that I can have a grouchy, touchy day without even knowing why. Dark, frosty mornings can cause it; a series of especially bad experiences at table can do it; a crowd of petty, nuisance-type, little things to take care of also suffices; facing hours or days of the most unpleasant aspect of my work will do it. But there are times when the reason for being grouchy is more elusive, and living doesn't really allow most of us hours and days to do a lot of navel-gazing. It would be nice if others would give you or me a wide berth at such times, but how are they to know before we snap for the first time?

Possibly these are times when we need to indulge some innocent appetite, like a hunger for chocolate muffins. Or maybe a little music would help. Talking to some understanding friend who can soothe us. Making plans for an outing or some entertainment. No, I haven't mentioned prayer yet. That could be helpful if we can bring ourselves to do so, even simply to complain. But it won't ordinarily work magic. As always, change and improvement comes about through an amalgam of grace and earthly help.

"If I should walk in the valley of darkness no evil would I fear." No matter how happy our life, how satisfying our job, how wonderful our mate or friends, most of us will walk in some dark valley at some time or other. The trust and peace of this most famous psalm (Ps 23) is inevitably tested if not shattered by some crushing moment. The anguished sentiments of Psalm 88 seem fit to be taken over wholeheartedly by any one of us at some time: "Lord my God, I call for help by day; I cry at night before you. . . . My soul is filled with evils; my life is on the brink of the grave." I feel "like those you remember no more." "You have taken away my friends. My eyes are sunken with grief. Lord, why do you hide your face?"

What might cause such anguish and despair is so personal, one hesitates to give examples. Betrayal or rejection by a friend or spouse; the grave illness or death of a child; the loss of a job; the unjust destruction of a reputation. . . . In such moments the words of a Psalm like 23 can be something to hang on to, something to keep hope alive in a bitter and crushed heart: "If I should walk in the valley of darkness no evil would I fear. Near restful waters you lead me, you revive my drooping spirit."

An unhappy and guilt-ridden spirit seems at times to be one response in the face of the infinite quantity of world suffering. If we can't change conditions for children working as slave laborers or for starving nations or victims of civil war, we can at least wipe the smile off our face and show everyone how seriously we take all this pain. Roberta Bondi writes of this useless approach to world suffering: "If the Christian did not have the guts to abandon a middle-class life in an overt way, then he or she could still demonstrate solidarity with those who suffered by internally rejecting ordinary life to live in a perpetual state of self-flagellating guilt" (*Memories of God*).[61]

The temptation is there. We feel that if we cannot here and now do anything about the mountain of human suffering, we can at least not appear to be happy. Possibly such approaches are driven by the right sentiments, but don't they simply add to the amount of hopelessness and discouragement in the world? Don't we who believe that Christ rose from the dead have to somehow combine the resulting hope and joy with whatever practical steps we can take for the alleviation of human misery?

Two pivots of our faith, as well as that of the Jews, are (1) the fact of God's loving care for us and (2) recalling that in a ritual celebration. The latter in the case of Christians is the Eucharist or Lord's Supper; in the case of the Jews, the Passover feast. As God prepared Moses for his role in the deliverance of his fellow Israelites from slavery, God said: "I am concerned about you and about the way you are being treated; so I have decided to lead you up out of the misery" (Exod 3:16). That God cares enough to deliver us from misery of whatever form is celebrated yearly in the feast of Passover. Jesus is our Moses, the one who has delivered us from slavery and misery. He says: "Come to me, all you who are weary and find life burdensome, and I will refresh you" (Matt 11:28).

We recall this invitation at the table of the Lord's Supper: "Do this in memory of me." Clearly, just coming to Mass does not guarantee the end of cancer, the lifting of depression, the settling of family feuding, an end to unfaithfulness. On the other hand, it is clear from Scripture that God is concerned to do something about our problems. Isn't it related to the fact that God is only able to work in us when we are receptive and, further, expect something from God? Why can't we trust in God's help at the same time that we call the doctor, consult the therapist, see the financial consultant, and work hard at overcoming our difficulties? God ordinarily works through us, through other human beings.

"I never realized how selfish I was." These were the words of twenty-five-year-old Bob in answer to a question about Sam, their/ his first child, now a year old. The focus of time and attention for

Kate and Bob is now on this little bundle of high maintenance. (This is all old hat for you older parents.) Those who so fear commitment must have an inkling that it will make demands they don't even want to think about (sleepless nights, diapers, topsy-turvy "dining"). Rearing Sam will demand of his parents an emptying of themselves reminiscent of Matthew 16:25: "For whoever wishes to save his life will lose it; but whoever loses his life for my sake will find it." St. Benedict gives that a very tough application in his Rule: "No one is to pursue what he judges better for himself, but instead, what he judges better for someone else" (RB 72.7). Possibly the people who decide matters like canonization will surprise us someday with "Saints Bob and Kate of Ourtown."

Will the loving care showered on little Sam build a deep conviction that God loves him?

Will this love result in confidence and a willingness to share that love with others?

Will that love perhaps reinforce the self-centeredness we may be acquainted with?

How do we reconcile freedom from self-centeredness with self-promotion to "get ahead" in our profession or business or with "fulfillment"?

Does having reared little dears explain why many older couples are so gracious and gentle compared to some of us crusty old celibates?

PS—Some septuagenarians and octogenarians claim to see vestiges of self-centeredness in themselves! Really! Perhaps all this points to our need for forgiveness and the grace and strength of the Savior Jesus Christ living in us.

Work or struggle or effort, none of these is the opposite of happiness. In fact, the more we live and reflect on living, the more we find that all three of them contribute to happiness. They are part of the odd mix that makes for contentment, peace, satisfaction. A life without work, challenge, one can even say some discomfort or antagonism quickly becomes insipid and dull. The opposite of happiness is probably meaninglessness or uselessness, rather than pain or effort. Something in us demands the opportunity to test our abilities and our strength. The fact that some sort of struggle, whether in a Bruce Willis film or in the account of St. Paul's travels, catches our attention, attests to how basic this is to our makeup.

It is hard to think of a compelling movie or story that doesn't involve someone facing obstacles and somehow resolving the situation. The winning young heroine must overcome parental objections; the knight must save the damsel locked up in the castle; the young man must conquer physical challenges to become a successful athlete. What might be most difficult for many of us is seeing how the daily, grinding effort and endurance that must go into our endeavor is ever going to lead to something better.

Some of these same stories can provide us with the encouragement to stay with it. In fact, the example of persistence over a long time in some cause is more likely to help us than some dramatic, one-time victory. Perhaps, we need look no further than our parents, our children, some of our friends, for instances of unsung persistence and faithful effort.

"Without music life would be a mistake." Possibly a bit overstated. But coming from a man, Friedrich Nietzsche, who had pretty well rejected the repressive Christianity of his youth, it's at least something. Music is assumed as part of worship throughout much of

Scripture and has had an immense place among Christians. What a difference a trumpet can make in the celebration of Easter or Christmas! The First Book of Samuel (16:14-23) tells of how King Saul was tormented by an evil spirit, which sounds a lot like what we would call bad moods. His attendants said they would look for "a man skilled in playing the harp" and that hearing him play would make him feel better. They found their harpist in multi-talented David. Whenever Saul was in one of his bad moods, "David would take up the harp and play, and Saul would be relieved and feel better for the evil spirit would leave him."

Music seems to be one of the most outstanding of God's gifts, clearly mediated through the talents of our fellow human beings. Prayer, medicine, talk, counseling—all have their place in overcoming our low spirits, our bad, even grouchy moods. But here's another help for many of us that, given how easily technology makes it available, seems obvious. The variety of music available to us on radio, on recordings should provide something appropriate for almost any human being who has ever responded to music. Music, I suspect, has fewer side effects than medication. A Christian could modify Nietzsche's phrase in a number of ways: "Life would be awfully miserable without music." "Life is harder to take without music." "Music is another way in which God touches us and gives us joy."

Mahatma Gandhi was asked once what he considered to be the essential teaching of Hinduism. He replied in words from a Hindu sacred book, the Isha Upanishad: "All this that we see in this great universe is permeated by God. Renounce it and enjoy it." Now, don't run away! I think there's something quite intelligible to all of us here and I hope to make that clear! Let me paraphrase the verse Gandhi quoted: All that we see around us in this great universe is filled with and penetrated by God. Let go of it; don't hold on to it possessively and then, enjoy it, appreciate it. More: the universe, all that is, belongs to and comes from God; God lives in it, in every part of it. It is not ours but it is definitely given to us to use and enjoy.

We enjoy it best by not seeking to take any part of it and make it our own private possession but by seeing it for its value, beauty, usefulness and approaching it accordingly. By letting go of it, by "renouncing" it, we try to let it be what it is as it comes from the hand of God. That means that all that is has a meaning and value apart from what I think it could be for me and I should try to see this. Letting go and enjoying is a bit like what parents must do with their grown children: be willing to let them be what they are or will become and then be able to appreciate the uniqueness that follows.

Someone has suggested the process of doing a crossword puzzle as a model for theology or for our understanding of life. She says it's "very arrogant to do it in pen." First you should do it in pencil since you'll probably find out something new that will require changing the original guess. Figuring out life might be like that too. At a certain cocky young age—or in a cynical phase—we think we've figured it out or, at least, seen through it and through other people. It's equally likely that at the same age, we find it all very confusing, making no sense. With age and experience, raising a family, working, we come to some certainties or near certainties. But these can be dashed or changed, too, by new experience. Sometimes we develop new answers to life's mysteries; other times we realize that there are no answers that are completely satisfying for some of these conundrums.

Our experience of trying to live a Christian life must tell us in regard to many matters that the best we can do—and it is the "best"—is to trust in the one who has shared our life and its puzzles and perils, Jesus Christ. "Lord God, you have called Your servants to ventures of which we cannot see the ending, by paths as yet untrodden, through perils unknown. Give us faith to go out with good courage, not knowing where we go but only that Your hand is leading us and Your love supporting us. . . . Amen."[62]

Life in the time of the psalmist seems to have been rough and chancy; it was either feast or fighting. On reflection, however, one must presume that between battle and bounty there were long stretches of routine and even boredom. But the Psalms seem to call on God almost exclusively in times of peril, distress, war, famine and sickness. The opening lines of Psalm 46, for instance, speak of God as our refuge or fortress, our help, in time of distress; it goes on to talk about trusting in God in the midst of what sounds like an earthquake. Many cultural differences have affected human life since the time of the psalmist. Apart from cancer, crime, and serious problems in relationships, doesn't it seem that for us today some of our calling on God is for help, endurance, and hope in the midst of boredom and a feeling of pointlessness?

Every event in our life is not of a magnitude to be measured on the Richter scale. Some of the situations in which we feel so down or listless are simply the buildup of routine. Of course, prayer and a good interior life are always a good recourse. But we should realize, too, that such dismal feelings can be the result of physical causes, treatable by the doctor; they can be due to lack of recreation, lack of physical activity in our life, lack of variety. Why not check these out, too, even as we ask God to be with us, to strengthen us, to give us more spirit and enthusiasm?

It was only a Tuesday evening when I overheard one student saying to another: "Have a good weekend." Whew! There are various explanations for the phrase, of course. Conceivably, she didn't know what day of the week it was. Or, she knew she wouldn't see the other till the following week. Or, we can take this kind of talk as typical of students who naturally grouse about school while, actually, having a pretty good time. Taking it at face value, though, it suggests that the Monday through Friday period is, if not intolerable, at least tedious. For many the work week is pretty awful: jobs are something to be suffered through in order to raise a family; for others who are more fortunate, they're interruptions of real life, an awful necessity.

Knowing the nature of the work some must do makes this understandable. Will it ever be otherwise? It looks like mindless, tedious, painful, boring, or simply uninspiring work will always be the lot of some. Of many? How we face at least forty of the most important hours of the week is important. Can we change our attitude toward our work? Can we think of finding something more congenial? Can anything be done about conditions? Does it make sense to see such a large part of our life as our cross, a kind of suffering from which we can draw some good? When you think of the fact that almost any work will have disagreeable aspects, perhaps it will help to see it as a sharing in the cross. "While we live we are constantly being delivered to death for Jesus' sake, so that the life of Jesus might be revealed in our mortal flesh. He who raised up the Lord Jesus will raise us up along with Jesus" (2 Cor 4:9-15 passim).

Physics talks about the law of the conservation of energy. There seems to be some law of the conservation of stress or pain or difficulty too. We pass a crucial exam for entrance into graduate school or for a promotion. Things seem more relaxed. Eventually some other stress comes. We pray and work for the health of an ailing mother. That is resolved. Things seem relatively quiet for a while. A cousin develops breast cancer. We share her fears through months of chemotherapy. She is in remission. We work and worry about our teenager's friends and habits during those years. Then her younger brother comes along with a new set of concerns. The children are all grown and on their own. Things are quiet on the home front. Then . . . ?

Rest and peace are never total or enduring. Each of us can draw all sorts of lessons and conclusions. Life is shaky; nothing can be taken for granted. Both sorrow and joy come and go. So many things are beyond our control. Everything is in God's hands. Our self-sufficiency is always provisional, even illusory. Possibly without the changes of fortune, the movement back and forth from stress to peace, pain to joy, difficulty to resolution, we'd be tempted to an unrealistic estimation of life. It isn't only at certain times that we need God; it's simply more obvious in the darker times.

Do we have to wait for priests, bishops, popes to launch initiatives? Are relations between various kinds of Christians to remain stagnant because the people at the top see all sorts of obstacles, real or not? When Jessie went through the windshield of her car in an accident and then back through it into the car with the resultant gashes and slashes and was comforted in the front seat by a stranger who stopped, he didn't ask what her faith was or what church she went to. Instead, he put his coat over her, held her hand, and prayed with her till help came. Like many a twenty-year-old college student, Jessie hadn't given prayer a lot of thought or attention. In the hospital, she was thankful to the point of tears for the person who sat and prayed with her in that life-threatening moment.

Eventually, she found out he was the pastor of a small rural church near her home town, a member of one of those groups that seem a little odd to mainstream Protestants and Catholics. You realize at such times that the big division among human beings is between those who trust in God and prayer and those who don't. A friend with a Christian background but who shows no signs of the practice of faith still thanks me for remembering him and his family in prayer. We'd be surprised at how many of our contemporaries appreciate or value prayer. Some willingness to express our trust in prayer could be, for those around us, their most inspiring and encouraging moment in their day or month.

That there are cycles in a marriage is probably no surprise to those married more than a few weeks. Mary Durkin names them this way: falling in love, settling down, bottoming out, and beginning again. They sound a lot like what happens in any serious, long-term commitment. My dictionary defines *bottoming out* rather dramatically as descending to the lowest point possible from which a new ascent might come. Chilling as that might sound to the young couple or the person joyously and generously embarking on a marriage or some enterprise, it seems realistic. It hardly seems possible that we can maintain unfailingly the enthusiasm with which we begin new commitments. We might maintain our responsibilities to the commitment; that I don't doubt, but the energy and excitement that we all love accompanying what we do is a different matter.

Prayer, Sunday Mass can become so blah, so heavy, such a drag. I doubt whether any one of us escapes this completely. For some, such periods might be very brief; for others, they might hang on like a chronic cold. Worse, the feeling might extend to everything in life: getting up in the morning, work, daily responsibilities. If we've "bottomed out" a number of times, we will probably realize that patience is partly what's needed. Unless these periods are of the type that require medical help, they will pass. Beginning again—and again—seems part of anything we ever want to preserve. Trusting that things can get better is part of their improvement. "At night there are tears, but joy comes with dawn," says the psalmist (Ps 30:6).

We believers in God might underestimate the difficulty God presents for some of our friends. The beauty of the Rockies or of a sunrise is clear evidence for some; the birth of a baby seems an obvious miracle; the existence of selfless people we meet and who have done us so much good is persuasive for some. St. Paul, too, thinks there is good evidence: "God's eternal power and divinity have become visible, recognized through the things he has made" (Rom 1:20). We're certainly justified in corroborating God's existence in our own way.

But others might not be convinced by the same things. There are emotional difficulties with believing, issues from our upbringing or experience that make it hard to believe, devastating events that we can't quite get over. Too, people might have very different ways of expressing their belief or of describing God. More familiarity with the Bible would show us a great deal of variety in how people think of God. God is always more than any one of us can say, always more than any one image. In the long run we point to God's existence and goodness better by how we live and act than by how we argue. Honing our arguments for God's existence is much less important than echoing God's love in what we do and say.

You wonder sometimes which is more disheartening: the content of television shows or the number of us who lie mesmerized by them. While there seems to be a proliferation of new sports or physical activities, you wonder if that just means there are more things one must watch. Are we more involved in life and the world around us or less? Critics of the age have pointed the finger at consumerism as our besetting vice. If it's not our own vice, it's certainly a temptation for all of us. If, along with consumerism, we take our willingness to be entertained rather than to do anything, we could name our chief vice passivity.

Counter to this is a spirit that sees life and its swiftly passing moments as opportunities to act, to do. An often quoted Irish toast goes: "May you live all the days of your life." Living here evidently means more than simply existing; it means we consciously use our moments, our breath, to do something more demanding than watching others get their exercise or simply taking in what technology offers. The people around us, from family to friends, especially benefit from our active interest and love, and, I suspect, most of us would feel some pulsating point to life, too, as a result.

The second of November is a sort of Christian Memorial Day; we remember the dead. No matter how we look on it, this day reminds us of them or of death. Unlike a fairly recent period in Christian history, we probably do not think primarily of the deceased as undergoing the pains of purgatory, away from the presence of God. Because of renewed attention to Scripture, we are more inclined to trust that God has forgiven and taken to the divine presence those who, though imperfect, put their confidence in God's love. With St. Paul in Romans we say: "If God is for us, who can be against us? Is it possible that he who did not spare his own Son but handed him over for the sake of us all will not grant us all things besides? . . . I am certain that neither death nor life, neither the present nor the future, will be able to separate us from the love of God that comes to us in Christ Jesus our Lord" (Rom 8:31-39).

It honors the love God has for us and lives up to the trust God asks if we confide the deceased to God's loving care. It further honors that love if we ourselves live in trust and confidence in God's forgiveness and love. Recalling those gone before us can arouse our thanksgiving for all they meant to us. Recalling that they have left our world urges us to live generously this short but precious time.

We all require some support for our faith in God. At some time in our life, we will ask or be asked by life and circumstances why we continue with prayer, Sunday worship, even the attempts to follow our consciences. The experience of a medical student in his mid-twenties might be that of many. He writes: "My experience of growing up within the Catholic faith was superficial at best. My parents were involved in my understanding of religion only to the extent that they made sure I was dropped off once a week for instruction. We never discussed religion or faith. Grace at meals was totally mechanical, as was going to church on Sundays. Whether or not we did anything while we were there was never an issue. 'You're supposed to go to church every Sunday.' That was the answer to any question. I love my parents dearly but I can't practice what I see as their religion or faith."

Very likely marriage to a committed Christian of another denomination and a lot of exposure to the scientific method helped trigger his reflections on faith. Whatever the resolution, we cannot expect that a saving faith can be merely something mechanical that we have inherited along with a Toro lawn mower or our nearsightedness. Our mind and heart have to be involved. Our thought and our will must play a part in it. After a lot more questioning, the writer was worried about consuming my time and energy with this problem. "Please don't let this letter worry or consume you. Remember, ultimately it is my responsibility." That's true for all of us.

"Why all this praising of God in hymns and prayers? We're not telling God anything God doesn't know." That was the complaint of a recent convert to Christianity. Another, after hearing the hymn "How Great Thou Art," said: "Why tell God how great God is? He knows that." Those of us who willingly worship and sing and pray such phrases may take all this for granted. For some, it is a problem.

The immediate response is that I praise and thank God for life itself, for my existence, first of all. After that, for the life, death, and resurrection of the Lord, which give me so much hope amid all the horrors of earthly existence. We hope, additionally, that most of us have family and friends whose love seems such a gift! To thank and praise God presumes we do not take all this for granted, that we know it is unearned, no matter how mediated through our parents and biology, through friends. Something we have not ourselves produced. Think of how, as little children, our parents had to educate us to gratitude. They said repeatedly: "Now what do you say?" It's doubtful that little children spend their break at day care speculating about where it all came from—the loving care of parents and all the goodies they enjoy. While self-evident to many, the necessity of praising and thanking God likewise has to be learned by reflection and probably a certain amount of experience. Without these, it is possible for some to say to themselves: life, existence; it's just here.

Truly, God does not need our praise. We need it; we need it as the appropriate response to our recognition that we, that life, all this is a gift. The alternative is simply that, consciously or not, we believe we are owed all this or that we ourselves produced it. Further, without praise from us for God, we risk becoming even more self-centered and self-indulgent. If God is not the center of our universe, who is? The other big contender is inevitably "me."

The four college student panelists on "Immigration and the American Dream" spoke about their experiences and that of their families in coming to the United States. The four were from Ukraine, the Hmong community, El Salvador, and Somalia. In detailing the hardships and the successes they and their families had encountered in immigrating, they brought themselves and the audience to tears at times. To close, the moderator asked them: "What would success mean to you?" The Hmong student said it would mean being able to provide a house for her parents where they could welcome the wider family. For the Salvadoran student it was similar: to be able to provide some measure of the "American dream" in the shape of a comfortable home for his parents after such experiences as sleeping in a fish processing factory or their car.

The soft-spoken young Somali Muslim said unabashedly and simply: "Success for me means living for others." That, of course, was implicit in the remarks of the other panelists. But the generosity of the statement was stunning. He went on to specify his hope of becoming a doctor able to bring medical care to people without it. "Living for others"—it brings us Christians back to the most demanding and difficult words of Jesus: lose your life in order to find it; give what you have to the poor and come, follow me; unless you deny yourself you cannot be my disciple. Selflessness as an ideal seems alive and well outside the Christian faith.

Late fall in my part of the world, before the snow falls, offers a very spare, austere landscape. The trees, except for the stubborn oaks, have lost their leaves; the grasses are various shades of pale yellow and brown. On a cloudy day the whole scene is of muted, somber colors, beautiful in its own subdued way. If one is in the right mood, all this can be appreciated. It's conducive not only to contemplation but also, for some, to a moment of melancholy. A good setting in which to re-read the Old Testament book of Ecclesiastes. Perhaps a good time to allow ourselves a more somber mood or a few minutes to experience some of the poignancy and beauty of human existence.

After all, human life has both tragic and happy aspects. Rather than simply brushing aside the former, we should at times give it some attention. With Ecclesiastes we can wonder about, even lament, the injustice that is evident; we can reflect on how difficult it is to change that and other things that are wrong; we can be sorry to see the really tragic things that happen to innocent people. It seems better to spend these melancholy moments with a book like Ecclesiastes and with God in prayer than to inflict them on otherwise happy people around us.

Faces! What variety! Variety in bone structure, eyes, hair, expression, smiles, mouths! And as the races intermingle through marriage, so many new variations! When we first meet another, it's the face we scrutinize; it's the face by which we most often try to remember all those people we met at the cocktail party. The more you think about it, the more amazing it is that the face with its expressions can tell us so much—or, at least, that we can read so much there. There are faces the sight of which can transform a day or bring light to the moment, faces we long to see again and again, faces that bring back memories. Faces that cause our own face to light up.

The psalmist prays: "O God, be gracious and bless us and let your face shed its light upon us" (Ps 67:1). Where else would a sacred writer get the idea of referring to the face of God if not from wonderful experiences of human faces? God sheds his light upon us most often through those human faces—dear, tender, beautiful, strong—whatever they may be to us. God looks at us with the assurance that we are loved most clearly through the faces of those who show us love. The Old Testament priestly blessing tells it all: "The Lord bless you and keep you! The Lord let his face shine upon you, and be gracious to you! The Lord look upon you kindly and give you peace!" (Num 6:24-26).

Flesh and spirit in St. Paul's writings seem dangerously close to what we call body and soul. He says, for instance: "If you live according to the flesh, you will die; but if by the spirit you put to death the evil deeds of the body, you will live" (Rom 8:13). But St. Paul is not talking about our familiar division of the human being into a material part and an invisible, spiritual part. Living according to the flesh here means a life focused on the world's values; where appearance and flash are valued more than substance; money and position over goodness and gentleness. To live by the spirit means to live and act in love, patience, generosity, forgiveness, and compassion. The great danger in taking his language to mean body and soul is that we end up thinking of the body as something bad and the spirit as good.

Genesis 1 tells us that everything God made is good. Despite this, Christians have all too often acted as if the body were somehow the delinquent party in the human person. Why would God have gone to the trouble of raising Jesus from the dead if the body was so negligible and unworthy? The body, like the materials used in the sacraments, contributes to our life in Christ. Through it we do others good; through it we cheer and comfort others. Through the body and such earthly things as music and the arts, we praise God and make visible something of God's goodness. Through the body of Christ (e.g., the Eucharist) we are joined to God and to each other.

In Luke's Gospel there is the story of a very short man, Zacchaeus, who climbed up a sycamore tree to catch a glimpse of Jesus. It is used in the church as an appropriate Gospel reading when we celebrate the anniversary of the completion of a church building. When Jesus saw Zacchaeus, he said to him: "Hurry down. I mean to stay at your house today." Zacchaeus was a wealthy tax collector and accordingly suspected of ill-gotten gain. The locals "murmur." Luke says: "He has gone to a sinner's house as a guest" (Luke 19:1-10).

Churches are buildings we human beings put up as places in which to honor God, reminders of God's presence with us. They are primarily our creation and serve our needs, definitely the houses of sinners in that sense. We might say they are places where God's compassion meets human need and sinfulness.

God's love and mercy meet human emptiness and sin in the church building. To those for whom the "bottom line" is everything, church buildings must seem a profound waste of space and means. But probably even more than we need such other "useless" things as music and art, we need a place for worship, a visible reminder of the invisible God. The church building says of itself that God is with and among us, that like his Son, God is profoundly interested in us sinners. Like Zacchaeus, we are hosts to the Lord in the church building and outside of it, too, insofar as we serve our fellow human beings.

"There is great grief and constant pain in my heart" (Rom 9:1).

St. Paul writes of the disappointment he feels that his people have not embraced belief in Christ. We hear the same pain and grief expressed in our time by parents who say: "We raised the kids as good Christians; we tried by good example and without being tyrants to lead them to Christ. But none of them goes to church; they aren't raising their children in the faith." It pains them to see what they regard as so important being rejected by their offspring. Neither Paul nor we can force the wills and choices of others. What we can and must do is trust in the value of our commitment and not let such disappointments lessen our generosity or good spirit.

We have been blessed with closeness to God and Christ, with life in the body of Christ, and with the assurance and strength this brings. Rather than wailing over what isn't and dreaming of some other time, we need to give the present our best, our gifts, our hope. Whining, nagging, complaining, self-pity, grumpiness, bitterness, silence are not, as Paul would say, the fruits of the spirit but of the flesh, of a short-sighted attitude. Rather, our true following of Christ shows itself in joy, kindness, forgiveness, respect for others' conscience, trust for the future, perseverance in prayer and worship. All that easily has unseen effects on others.

The rejection by so many, then and now, of the one who came to bring God's message of love makes you wonder about God's methodology. Why such a chancy way of doing it, appearing in the form of an ordinary man, the son of a local carpenter? Why not paint the message in bright and bold colors across the skies for everyone to see? If God made this vast universe, it certainly wouldn't have been a tiring task to do this. In one part of the sky it could have been in Russian, in another in Arabic, elsewhere in English, and so on. But no, God seems to make it purposely difficult by tying the revelation of divine love to acceptance of a fellow human being.

That really underlines a fundamental truth about God's relation to us. We cannot be related honestly in love to God without a willingness to accept and love our fellow human beings. We only truly accept God's love if we are willing to see God's love there, to accept assurances of God's love for us in the good actions and care of others. The other side of this, equally important, is that others will know God really loves them if someone cares for them in their loneliness, their need, their pain, their discouragement and fear, their hunger and homelessness. At the altar in Communion, we become Christ's body in order to be Christ to and for others.

Conceivably, some people are "naturally" cheerful as we say; but happiness, a deeper reality, is not simply a matter of temperament. It is partly our choice and partly the by-product of something else good that we are doing. It's a choice insofar as we can choose how we look at life, how we respond to its hardships and heartbreaks, its delights and joys. If we start with the basic premise that life itself is a gift, not something we produced, we have a basis for looking at everything with thanksgiving. And the result of that is happiness. If we start with the opposite premise—that everything we have and are and even more is owed to us—we're sure to be unhappy.

Further, happiness is the by-product of work well done, life well lived, love and appreciation generously given. "My opinion," ancient Chinese writer Chuang Tsu says, "is that you never find happiness till you stop looking for it." Someone else put it like this: take care of truth, goodness and love, and happiness will take care of itself, will come of itself. Pursuing happiness itself usually means chasing entertainment. "Life, liberty and the pursuit of happiness" is a well-known phrase from the American Declaration of Independence. Forgive my presumption, but I think the "pursuit" part is misleading. Genuine happiness can be ours independently of a search for excitement and variety; it's something much deeper in us that can coexist with surface trials and worries.

Famous for popular songs like "Margaritaville," Jimmy Buffett responded to the suggestion that he might be the world's greatest party person: "I was! I had a great time! Then people start dying, you know. And having nervous breakdowns. And then you go, 'Wait a minute here.' "[63] His comments, of course, are familiar: death, disease, and tragedy bring us all up short. But the timing is interesting. Suddenly, at this late date, we say to ourselves: "People are dying and having nervous breakdowns." "People" here seems to mean people I went to school with or who were in my wedding or with whom I worked or played basketball. Others' deaths, disease, and tragedy get to us when they hit close.

Ultimately, even these have a tough time competing with the impact of "my" death, "my" illness, "my" personal tragedy. They tell us as they told Buffett, "Wait a minute here." The lesson is obvious and old but now is as good a time as any to pause. We're rushing about, up to our ears in deadlines. Am I shortchanging these people around me who are or will be dying, getting sick, having breakdowns? Can I put aside my work, my worries, my ambitions enough to be with my husband or wife, children, friends? *Be Here Now* was the title a sixties guru gave to his book celebrating an insight he derived from Hinduism. However we come to it, we need to "be here now."

There they were, the same crowd, friends since high school (some even longer) and college, looking twice as handsome as people in their twenties ordinarily are, dressed up for the wedding of Jake and Kay, in exuberantly high spirits. Humans at their most radiant and attractive. Two months earlier the same people were all dressed up but feeling quite otherwise when they attended the funeral of John, another classmate and friend, who had been senselessly murdered by an intruder in his apartment.

You wonder what brings us together more, joy or sorrow? That might be impossible to answer. It is vital, though, to give ourselves to these moments, to join in them, for our own good and that of all the others. Shared joy and shared grief bind us together in a way that is irreplaceable by anything less. There should be no question about making time for grief—and for joy.

The Lord's harshest words in the Gospels are addressed to his religious opponents, especially the Pharisees (Matt 7:1-5). He calls them hypocrites to their face for their severe judgment of others. His angry comments might make us forget that the line between hypocrites and good people doesn't run clearly and cleanly between the Pharisees and ourselves. The Pharisees weren't, in fact, simply hypocrites; they were Jews attempting to be faithful to the Law who had lost sight of its purpose in the process. The resulting self-righteousness is a temptation for many religious people. We are all warned—in the Pharisees—against usurping God's position as judge. It helps greatly to avoid this by looking first at ourselves. Honestly seeing our own faults limits our willingness to condemn others.

Over and over again, we see how those who rant most fervently against vices are tripped up by the same vices. The preacher who holds up the Bible on TV and condemns sexual license is shown to be an adulterer. There seems to be some psychological law involved which verifies so often that what we denounce most strongly is what we know only too well. "Clean up your own act" would be the contemporary way of putting the advice of Jesus to all of us who are tempted to judge. All of us who commune with the Lord and each other at the altar are also in solidarity with each other in sin and the need for forgiveness and understanding.

"You crown the year with your goodness.
Abundance flows in your steps;
in the pastures of the wilderness it flows.
The hills are girded with joy,
the meadows are covered with flocks,
the valleys are decked with wheat.
They shout for joy, yes, they sing"
(Ps 65:12-14).

Singing of a bountiful harvest like this is understandable in much of the American Midwest or in some other breadbasket of the world. At times, of course, drought, flood, or frost may limit that, but usually fall is quite bountiful. Praying or reading these words, though, one must think of how inapplicable they are to some land plagued for years by drought, war, or flood. What do we do? Should we be satisfied to think that there are inequalities, injustices? And that we must accept them; it's simply good or bad luck?

The more we are aware of how we form one world, one universe (one is actually redundant here), even one huge organism, the more we must realize how offensive is this huge inequality. Communication, technology, our whole modern world make possible almost instant presence to others, to other places and peoples; they make possible massive movements of anything we wish to move. What prevents us from assuring that the whole world shares in the blessings of harvest time is not know-how but a willingness to do it. We can work for that or contribute to that in our own fairly obvious ways. Somehow we and our world can do better at sharing the loaves and the fishes.

Psalm 39 is full of poetic expressions of the shortness of life:
> You have given me a short span of days;
> my life is nothing in your sight.
> A mere breath, the one who stood so firm;
> a mere shadow, the one who passes by;
> a mere breath, the hoarded riches—and who will take them, no
> one knows. . . .
> In your house I am a passing guest—a pilgrim, like all my
> forebears.

The words, though they speak of the fragility of our life, still may have a bittersweet beauty for us. (The inevitability of decay adds urgency to our appreciation of spring and the beauty of nature.) We see the same fleeting character of all creation evidenced in the cycles of nature, in flowers, in the seasons, in every form of beauty. We see it, more close to home, in the sudden and/or accidental death of a young person.

But, no matter how much we take the words or events to heart, it is still difficult for us to really believe in our own decay and death. Rarely do such words, no matter how frail our physical being, prevent us from planning a winter getaway, from buying a new suit or having the roof replaced. We can perhaps speak feelingly of our mortality and the shortness of life, but to really imagine our own death seems almost impossible. A psychiatrist reports that he has rarely heard a patient say, "When I die"; more often it is, "If I die." Perhaps the best we can do is attempt to be more aware of how fleeting life is and more gently conscious of that in those around us.

At least in one medical school I've observed, students must spend a certain amount of time in a wheelchair to learn by experience what that entails. After some weeks of this experience myself, this seems eminently wise—not to mention irreplaceable. None of us can really know from hearsay, a lecture, or even observation what it's like to be confined to a wheelchair. You discover how inconvenient many objects and locales are for those who lack the powers of upright humans. You often become a non-person for the freestanding adult who looks right over you in a crowd and finds it hard to treat you as an equal. Others seem to think the condition contagious. It's both shocking and humbling. Not only physically but emotionally you feel below others. You often must ask them for help or excuse the fact that you take up more space.

One young man in a wheelchair says that originally he was so stubborn that it was difficult for him to ask. Now, he says, "Whenever anyone offers to push me or do anything else for me, I take it." You learn an almost childlike quality, the necessity of asking for many services and objects, if not everything. Perhaps not just medical students but all of us should have the experience of being in a wheelchair for at least a few days, better yet, a week. It might give more flesh and blood to our efforts to practice the sensitivity which is love in practice. It wouldn't be so much a matter of walking in another's shoes, as riding in another's wheelchair.

The author of a book on science and religion says that most people find their security in personal relationships, not in principles, politics, philosophies, wealth, science, or even a book like the New

Testament. When it comes down to it, we put our trust in people, individuals, friends, spouses. What's wrong with these other things? Possibly it's that they are so impersonal, unfeeling, unresponsive; ideas, principles, cosmic events—none of them will hold you in their arms when you're convulsed with grief or totally make up for a day of harsh encounters. No one ever sang, "You'd be so nice to come home to" to a concept.

The New Testament looks at the partners in marriage as reflecting for each other the unending, unconditional love Christ has for us. We know, best of all from our own experience, that there are people who do this, who are this for another or for others. The experience of the faithfulness of another brings down to earth the love God has for us, in fact, puts flesh on that love. Not to forget: our faithfulness and reliability, our constancy to others, these do the same for them.

In the north central United States, we often have abundant snow in wintertime. For children and the young in heart, it's always exciting, something new and usually unexpected. It means winter sports, playing in the snow, snowball fights, a world transformed into a white wonderland. For many older and/or jaded people, it means only difficulty in getting around and snow removal. Unfortunately, even allowing for people's preferences about weather and winter, we tend to bring the same yawn and boredom to other more undeniable gifts and surprises in life.

Why do we stop being excited by a great smile? A lively and exhilarating personality? A beautiful face or handsome appearance? Is it a sign of greater sophistication that we allow ourselves to be bowled over only by very expensive or rare things and aren't fazed by the miracles of daily life? Is there some peer pressure that requires we leave enthusiasm and great delight for the young and naive, which says it is unbecoming in those of more experience? Unapologetic enjoyment is a great good, really a praise of God, the source of all our good. Do we allow it into our lives?

It sounds exaggerated and we could dismiss it as just another example of religious hyperbole: "In God alone is my soul at rest; from God comes my help. God alone is my rock, my stronghold, my fortress; I stand firm" (Ps 62:1-2).

In reality we find our rest, comfort, peace with friends or family; our help, too, comes from their support, from doctors, medicine, possibly even from the words of a stranger written in a book. It doesn't seem simply to come from God alone. Yet, when we put the help and support of all these along with God, we must admit that they can fail, through no fault of their own—or through their own fault. A friend can end a relationship; a dispute can take away support; illness, incapacity, and death can remove our earthly "rock" from us, no matter how faithful she has been. There is some point to giving attention purely to God, apart from all those who mediate that grace and goodness to us.

"God alone is my rock, my stronghold, my fortress; I stand firm."

Many "human potential" movements emphasize that all that is wonderful, encouraging, and joyous can be found within ourselves. They make a valuable point about how we so easily leave our potential unused. Christian faith does not deny this but points also to all there is outside ourselves for which we can be thankful. That means starting with our creation by God and the whole creation that surrounds us, from heavens to humans. It means the love of God shown us further in the salvation and promises given us in Christ.

Each of us has her or his own list of items for which to be thankful. We can start at the outer edges of this vast universe or begin in the depths of our own being. Either way, our life, our existence is a fabric of gifts, items whose origin was not our doing. Especially those of us in relatively good health, living a comfortable existence in a much blessed country, have no excuse for whining and complaining. As the chronically ill and the poor so often teach us to our embarrassment, there are so many things, so many people, so many events for which we should be thankful. We'd do well to list for ourselves all the gifts that make our life so livable—and more.

Is the subject of miracles bound to be obscure, incomprehensible? Is there anything that can be said that is at all satisfying? After pursuing the subject in any number of books of theology meant for us ordinary mortals, I'm inevitably left unsatisfied. That itself may be telling me something worthwhile: that miracles are not something you or I are going to figure out with our reason. Perhaps the central thing about them is that they are not able to be contained within the thoughts and science we have developed. Writers in effect try to explain them away or offer some partial but basically unsatisfactory explanation. We don't know at this stage of human development—and probably never will—what are all the laws of nature. To say that a miracle is an exception to those laws is no help.

Discuss the topic with thoughtful believers and they will bring up examples of miracles without being any closer to defining them. They will tell us how their father was freed from cancer by the prayers of family and friends. How the seemingly hopeless case of a friend paralyzed in an accident was turned around and she is now up and walking. Faith in prayer and in God's care for us is what finds miracles, what sees miracles. We can and should continue to think about miracles but, better yet, leave God space in which to act in ways beyond our comprehension. Even apart from what we might think of as miraculous, the results of continuous prayer can be surprising.

In reading these reflections, you have probably noticed my veneration of parents for the patience they show in rearing their children. Seeing a mother or father continue shopping and keeping a smile on their face as their little one emits screams heard all over the supermarket leaves me awestruck. They are learning or have learned enough patience to qualify for sainthood. Joan Pierce, a reader of these reflections, suggests another angle to this. Though her qualifications may be a bit exceptional—she is the mother of eight—and now old enough to see her husband showing symptoms of Alzheimer's, she gives us much to think about. With her permission and a little editing, I quote some remarks of hers on the subject.

"I was a mother of eight children and you'd think I would have learned patience. But instead I learned how to fit a lot of needs and wants into a busy schedule while urging us all to 'hurry up.' . . . Ten years ago, my husband began to show symptoms of Alzheimer's. I didn't worry about patience then, but watched and tried to cope. Now I have ALS and I find time to be patient. Patient with all the slow old people who react almost as slowly as I do. Patient with all the fast-paced younger ones who want to help. Patient with myself."

"And He will raise you up on eagle's wings,
bear you on the breath of dawn."[64]

We often hear this sung at funerals; we are praying that the deceased
friend will now be freed from all that weighed her down. But in-
stinctively we feel that our faith should refresh us even now, put a
spring in our walk, free us a bit from the pull of gravity. Heaviness,
dragging along as if we were carrying all the world's burdens on
our backs—all this strikes us as at least not ideal. Shouldn't we feel
a youthful urge to run, buoyed by the strength of God? The Lord
says his yoke is easy and his burden light (Matt 11:28-30). Shouldn't
we at times feel able to "soar with eagles' wings"? "They that hope
in the Lord will renew their strength" (Isa 40:30).

Some of the saints demonstrate that God's grace, closeness to God,
can be a greater motivator than a dozen motivational speakers.
Perhaps more reflection, more hope and expectation would make
the strength of the Lord flow over into our daily life. We all feel
drained at times, maybe continually so, but is there anything wrong
with asking the Lord to give us some of that refreshment he has
promised? "My yoke is easy and my burden light." The Lord whose
coming we prepare for is already present and with us, the more so
as we trust. In the word of the Lord, in the bread and wine of the
altar, the Lord's power, love, and strength are present to put life into
our plodding legs, to inspire more smiles, to restore some youth.

"You cannot give yourself to God and money" (Luke 16:13). After
hearing this from Jesus, Luke tells us, the Pharisees "began to
deride him." Probably no other Gospel records so much opposition
between the teaching of Jesus and our concern for material goods.
We might not "deride" Jesus, but we certainly feel at times that this
railing about the dangers of wealth is a bit exaggerated. Jesus,

however, is unrelenting on the issue and, anticipating our objections, says: "What man thinks important, God holds in contempt" (v. 15). Our values and those of our society are not God's.

In our day, a similar message comes to us from those who warn us against unrestrained consumerism, against the irresponsible use of our world's resources. (Hear Francis!)

One way to begin to enter into this teaching of Jesus would be to think of what we could get along without rather than looking for ways to accumulate things. (I know this is certainly a counter-cultural approach!) Some would put it, "Small is beautiful" or "Less is more." Such attitudes are not only good for our world, our universe, but can help us to turn our attention and energy to the life within, to life in Christ, to our relation to God. "What we think important, God holds in contempt."

How do you tell a rut from a tradition? That seems to be a genuine problem for an institution as old as the Catholic Church—and many others—as well as for smaller units with strong customs. In an institution like the church, we can surmise that a tradition has become a rut when it drives people away, when it turns off a generation. It has become a rut when no one seems to know why we continue it or what it means.

"The Church can . . . come to see that certain customs not directly connected to the heart of the Gospel, even some which have deep historical roots, are no longer properly understood and appreciated," Francis, the Bishop of Rome has said. He continues: "Some of these customs may be beautiful, but they no longer serve as means of communicating the Gospel. We should not be afraid to re-examine them. At the same time, the Church has rules or precepts which may have been quite effective in their time, but no longer have the same usefulness for directing and shaping people's lives."[65]

There are probably such ruts in our personal lives, activities or habits that take up time and are merely routine without doing much for anyone. One way to simplify and reinvigorate our life might be to prune it of such mechanical practices.

We can only use the Psalms as prayers for ourselves if we're willing to let pass some of the more distasteful or incomprehensible elements we meet there. The authors call down God's rage on their opponents; we don't have to. We don't have to remind God of all the "great things" we have done. But we can find in the Psalms many a phrase which can serve as a theme for the day, an expression of what we hope for: "The Lord is my strength and my salvation." "In you, O Lord, I trust." Or, what often strikes me in Psalm 51:14: "With a spirit of fervor sustain me" and right before that, "Give me again the joy of your help."

That last verse might be good to pull out when one feels less than excited about the upcoming day, work, or other matters. We can, of course, do simply natural human things that enliven or galvanize. But repeating these phrases as a sort of mantra might help to change the attitude or mood. "Give me again the joy of your help." Help me, Lord, to be grateful for my life and work and to show it by my spirit, by some joy. Despite an occasional bad or less-than-fervent mood, we may be able to recall some happy elements within, e.g., a generally very happy life, good work to do, and wonderful people to work with. A little reflection may bring up thoughts of my good fortune relative to many others, urge me to show some goodwill and love to all those around me. We could end up thinking there is really no serious reason for not feeling grateful and even joyous.

Let me not waste the day, my time in listlessness, aimlessness, boredom, lassitude. Help me face each moment, each task, each person I encounter with enthusiasm and appreciation, with my whole heart and strength. Help me to be fervent rather than frightened, generous rather than grumbling, hopeful rather than fatalistic, encouraging rather than dispiriting, eager rather than tepid. "With a spirit of fervor sustain me, Lord."

While praying in the garden the night before his suffering and death, Jesus said to the disciples: "Wait here and watch with me" (Matt 26:38). He didn't send them off to importune the local bureaucrats for another hearing, to get reinforcements, or to organize a protest. Many a contemporary of ours would consider his words too passive; why not tell them to do something rather than just wait and watch? It is difficult for people raised in our culture just to sit and watch. We feel we're being judged by our peers on how proactive we are, how able to do something. Part of Jesus' point is that in some circumstances the best thing to do is to wait, watch, be present.

The friends of Job who harangued him in his suffering finally did the right thing when they shut up and sat with him in his misery. The words of Jesus admonish us to question the value of our frenzied activity. We are so busy getting somewhere that we often have no time to be anywhere. In our pursuit of education or of advancement, of business opportunities, we need to learn just to be, to be present to those who need us. Our silent presence cannot have a price put on it; yet it's often worth more than our fumbling actions. "Wait and watch."

Things like sleep shouldn't prevent us from seeing—at least once in a while—a clear, starry sky either at night or early in the morning. That sight cannot be replaced by anything we might read or, even less, see on TV. To let ourselves get lost in wonder at the vastness of the universe, the incredible number of stars, the distances is both humbling and expansive.

Can't we draw, depending on the occasion, some conclusions from this? For instance, that some of my concerns and problems are pretty silly, really not worth our whining or worry. Or, the sight can suggest the immensity of God that in turn points to God's capacity to handle our difficulties and problems, to bring order and beauty out of our lives. Some, of course, will be tempted to think that a God of such vastness cannot really be concerned about me, my sorrows and worries. But Christ has to come into any Christian view of the universe, and the existence of the Son of God in human flesh tells us that God does care, is not so crippled by huge concerns that we and our problems are beneath God's concern.

Psalm 147 has these verses one after the other:
God heals the broken-hearted,
and binds up all their wounds.
God fixes the number of the stars;
and calls each one by its name.

In my part of the world in mid-December the sun rises not too long before eight and sets a bit after four. If the weather is quite mild—that is, hanging around the freezing point—we're likely to have a cloudy day also. Information about when the sun rises and sets has to be taken on faith, one might say. We often don't actually see it. At this same time of the year, the Advent texts read in church seem most appropriate: "Though darkness cover the earth and thick clouds the peoples, upon us the Lord shines" and "A people living in darkness has seen a great light; on those overshadowed by death a light has arisen."

Christ is that light, the Son of God come in the flesh. If those around us are to sense that the Lord does offer illumination, brightness, warmth, that will certainly require faith on their part. But we ease it for them, we bolster the faith of others, if some of that light shines out in our behavior. If some hope, joy, and confidence are apparent in what we do and say. The light of the Lord only becomes actual, meaningful for our world through the illumination, warmth, and raising of spirits that Christians bring with them.

Ignorance plays a part in our decisions, our actions. Not only what we know about a place we're going to or a job we're taking, but what we don't know often ends up being quite significant. Some things we don't know in advance because we don't think to ask or don't have even enough knowledge to know what to ask. Some ignorance is based on just too narrow a perspective; if we aren't comparing the heat and humidity of a particular city with the fresh and crisp climate of another, it might be for lack of a wide-enough angle in our camera.

Should we spend more time, more study in trying to see all angles before ever acting or moving? That could be pretty stultifying, enough to stop us in our tracks for a long time. Our ignorance is another word for the inevitable risk involved in so many things we undertake. Not knowing all the difficulties in advance is good in the long run. We grow into an ability to deal with elements that, if foreseen, might have frozen us into immobility. Some lack of knowledge, some obscurity, the unknown—these are all part of life, of the next moment. Accepting that is another part of accepting that we are not "masters of the universe," that we depend on and come from Another.

Vigilance. Alertness. Readiness. They're admirable and we appreciate them in our fellow workers, friends, and those close to us, but being prepared for anything is often where we so easily fail because of procrastination, laziness, or simple weariness. We fall in love without thinking. We take off for a vacation in Mazatlán only to find we've packed a parka and forgotten sunscreen. So often we're not ready because we're not really here. We waste time by being only half present, like the disquieting experience of being at dinner or in a conversation with someone only to see that he or she is looking beyond us for something or someone else.

Someone has put it memorably: "Nothing is so rare as the moment when we want to be where we are, doing what we are doing." Attention, being truly present, is what can transform even the simplest moments of life. The present and what we are doing deserves more respect. Our talk gives away how little we prize the present: We "catch" a bus; "grab" a bite to eat; "dash off" a letter or a report; "run" to the store; "get through the week." But this present moment and place are where God and others are, where real life is. Diana Eck says: "Just being awake, alert, attentive is no easy matter. I think it is the greatest spiritual challenge we face. Finally, I think, it is the only one."[66] Could be.

After years of looking for someone else to blame for all our deficiencies, there seems to be more appreciation today of accountability and responsibility. In fact, the former word may be in danger of taking its place with other overexposed words like *diversity* and *codependency*. This new trend could encourage us to see the value of our life, our words, our example for our family, our friends, our neighborhood, our world. What we do or do not voluntarily do in the way of worship, love, honesty does strengthen or weaken the character, the tone, the texture of the community of which we are part.

For our little part of the world and for many people around us, we are irreplaceable; without the things we do or say, they are diminished. Our lives, words, and actions can build up or tear down. Our encouraging words or gestures help someone else through the day—or the night. Our sympathy and listening tell others they are not alone, have worth. The respectfulness or dignity we bring to what we do helps others believe in the worth of living. What we do in response to our conscience is vital to the world around us and is our way of responding to the call of the Lord in the here and now.

"Be watchful, pray constantly, that you may be worthy to stand before the Son of Man" (Luke 21:36).

This essential Advent theme would, of course, fit any time of the year. Sudden deaths of people in their prime, of young people, the appearance of cancer in ourselves or a loved one—all these remind us to live more mindfully, with more awareness of what life is and is all about. In the same context as the opening line, Jesus says, "Be on guard lest your spirits become bloated with indulgence and drunkenness and worldly cares" (v. 34). We hear often about the good of simplifying our lives, and usually we mean getting rid of unnecessary possessions, objects. In what we've just quoted from Jesus is reference to another form of this: Be on guard against worldly cares.

We need to make sure our vision of what is important in life, what we are living for is clear. The worries and concerns of human life can obscure our vision and our purpose. A sixteen-year-old with cancer or the loss of a job for those who support a family, these are legitimate cause for concern and, it is to be hoped, for constant prayer. But worldly care means our anxiety about keeping up with fashions or the neighbors, our fussing about the nonessentials of life. These we can profitably forget in order to reduce the clutter in our lives, to help us focus on what life is really about.

Who are you kidding? Are you joshing me? (An expression we Americans use meaning are you teasing me? Or, you can't be serious!) This could be an honest response to the Advent phrase "Come, Lord Jesus!" or any similar references to the coming of Christ. Our more thoughtful response might be: "I'm praying for the Lord to come now? I'm not ready! My life is a mess: ill-will toward others, abuse of sex, too much drinking, up to my neck in debt, etc." Or, "I'm pretty conscientious but my focus is on family, people I love and who love me. I enjoy food and drink, travel, parties, dancing, music, sports. I'm still hoping to see Reykjavík. I try to honor and even love God by the way I treat others, but I'm not ready to leave all this."

The Coming can refer to the end of everything, to my death, or to the Lord's coming in Christmas. The latter is quite a bit more cozy and comforting than thinking of the other two. Christmas reminds us of the manger, the angels and shepherds, and all this mingled with snowflakes, mulled wine, and sleigh rides. In the manger we have a child, come to live and share our life, even its worst suffering, to show God's love. The coming of the Lord can also refer to his presence in Scripture and Sacrament and in our fellow worshipers at the Eucharist. That again is easier to take: but coming to a roll up of creation or to my death? That's another matter.

But meeting the Lord as we pray, sing, and take Communion with other believers can help us prepare for that final coming. Some personal prayer during the silences at Mass can help us develop a greater trust in God's love for us. That can help us face death with less fear and think of it more as a return to the loving God who gave us life and all it holds in the first place, who waits to receive us back. "O come, Divine Messiah, / The world in silence waits the day / When hope shall sing its triumph, / And sadness flee away."[67]

To be or not to be. To do or not to do. To commit ourselves or not to commit ourselves. The doubts and questions of Hamlet are those of all of us. There are so many variations on the theme of commitment. We have the story in the Gospel about the two sons. One says Yes to his father's order and never carries it out; the other says No but afterward goes and carries it out anyway (Matt 21:28-32).

By our baptism, by prayer, public profession of faith, regular worship we formally say Yes to God. In that, we're like the chief priests and elders among Jesus' people; they formally subscribe to the Covenant with God. Yet, Jesus with the story about the two sons tells them that the sinners, tax collectors, and prostitutes are really more faithful to what God asks than they. Commitment has to go beyond words and gestures to how we treat the poor and unloved, the suffering and needy, any who have a claim on us. The Yes we utter in church needs an echo in daily life and behavior.

Most of us at some idealistic moment of our life have had our ideals severely tested or even dashed by what we see in others—and maybe in ourselves. We've thought of the Christian community as a place of peace and goodwill, mutual concern, only to be hurt by a vicious tongue, a grouchy member of the parish team, or sexual exploitation by a pastor. If we know ourselves well, we may be able to rebound from some of these hurts as we recognize the same behavior in ourselves. The Christian faith presumes as a basic tenet that we are all deficient in some ways, that we all need healing and salvation.

Some of our shock may come from too little experience or lack of self-knowledge. The larger and more flagrant offenses against our ideals may require a lot of treatment and time, and cannot be minimized. The smaller, daily ways in which we let others down require forgiveness, looking at ourselves, and a continuance of realistic hope. We have to expect that others will get over and actually forgive our indifference, our flare-ups, our laziness, our loose tongue. Life could not go on if we or they simply accumulated and kept a file of hurts. Possibly this is where the idea of beginning each day anew comes in. Instead of carrying over to tomorrow the hurts of today, we try with God's help—and Christ's example!—to start with a new and clean slate.

Gift-giving at Christmas has been tarnished for some because of the consumerism and commercialism attached to it. Margaret Visser says that the lack of meaningful relationships in many people's lives leaves an emptiness that people try to fill with purchases: "Objects are simpler than people, shopping easier than conversation or attempts to understand others' needs."[68] But happily there are many who understand that giving echoes or reflects God's gift to us of God's Son. Our gifts—whether material, verbal, or of service—at least minimally symbolize some gift of self on our part. Simply put, Christians are happy that God became human in Jesus and in response want to give something from their happiness to others.

Giving, however it shows itself, is a reflection of God's gift of Jesus and much else. It stems from gratitude for many gifts: creation, our existence, our life and opportunities, all that family and friends mean to us, and much else special to each one of us. Giving gifts and sharing greetings can reinforce for the recipients the reality of God's love for them. And conversely, those who give should know that they and their giving are evidence of God's love. God's gift in the manger to all of humankind echoes throughout the year in all the signs we show of self-giving in our words and deeds.

"Other seasons are for getting ahead; this one is for enjoying where you are." That was an ad for Southern Comfort (sounds like some kind of blanket, doesn't it?). The last phrase is certainly true—enjoying where you are—not only during Christmastide but any time. All the seasons of the Christian year plead with us to give love now, to use our God-given talents, to be present where we are now. To realize how irreplaceable, how unrepeatable, this dinner, this paper, this person, this laughter, this time together is. Every season, really, tells us: write that letter today; call that friend this evening; begin that exercise program this morning.

We're not talking about frantic, frenzied "grabbing the gusto," but rather of dignifying and honoring everyone, every event, and every moment with attention, care, reverence—now. On a smaller scale, it's like the commitment we give to a husband or wife, that we hope for and expect in a marriage. Instead of looking over our shoulder continually for some fairy tale person, we give this person our undivided and loving attention. So, too, instead of spending couch-potato hours on remote, media celebrities, why not discover the abilities, skills, beauty of the people with whom we actually live and work? Enjoy, rather more, live where you are.

The book of Ecclesiastes not only corresponds to our more melancholy and low moods, it also shares our doubts and questions. The author looks around him and sees the injustice of the world. "I considered all the oppressions that take place under the sun: the tears of the victims with none to comfort them" (4:1). "And those now dead, I declared more fortunate in death than are the living to be still alive. And better off than both is the yet unborn, who has not seen the wicked work that is done under the sun" (4:2-3). He questions whether things are ever righted, living at a time when any idea of rewards and punishment in an afterlife was missing.

What he sees makes him wonder, if not doubt, about any good plan or purpose in the whole thing. Even we who have a belief in the resurrection and hope of eternal life might find the human picture at times very discouraging or find events in our life devastating to our faith. Over the centuries people have been shocked at finding this book in the Bible. Its somber mood and questioning seem so counter to the hope and trust we encounter elsewhere. The presence of such a questioner in the Bible tells us that doubts and questions about faith are not sinful. They might show, as they do with Ecclesiastes, that we take it seriously and hope to see more justification of our faith in ordinary life. We really only have doubts or questions about people and things that are very important to us. They attest to our love and faith and can help make them deeper.

The widow Anna (Luke 2:36-40), in her faithfulness to temple worship and prayer, reminds us of the many women who often form the core of the faithful at daily worship in our churches. The real guarantee of any virtue is perseverance in it, through thick and thin, in fervor or fatigue. Anna, Luke tells us, "was constantly in the temple, worshiping day and night in fasting and prayer." It's so much more attractive to us to do things by fits and starts, to pray by whim and feeling. The wisdom of an Anna is to a large degree the result of staying with it in dry periods and times of excitement, when our heart sings and also when it is heavy and seems like a rock. There are insights that come from constant attentiveness to God and prayer that cannot be gained from books or study. How do we stay with it when we feel utterly dead, dull, and indifferent? Simply by repeating, over and over again if necessary, to God some expression of our emptiness and need.

Those of us who are joined to Christ so frequently in Communion must wonder sometimes about what effect it has on us. We should expect that over time a sincere participation in the Lord's Supper should cause some transformation, should be making us more like him whose body and blood we share. One element that contributes to the effectiveness of this sacrament is the personal prayer which, in addition to that of the service, surrounds it. The full effect of Christ living in us cannot be realized apart from our personal engagement by prayer, our own unique conversation with Christ.

Communion is not fast food or magic. Our faith and prayer should express our trust that Christ can transform us. We are fed with this bread and wine, the Body and Blood of the Lord, in order to live as he does. In John 6 we read: "Just as the Father has sent me and I have life because of the Father, so you who feed on me will have life because of me." Genuine prayer and faith allow Christ to make us one with him, to transform us into the one body of Christ. Over time it should become easier for others to see Christ in and through us.

Jon's story (part one): Jon says of this story that it is "maybe a cautionary tale, but also a testament to God's grace and mercy." Even at five years of age living with his family in rural North Dakota, he knew he wanted to be a priest. Two years later the family moved to Minneapolis, where nuns and priests abetted that desire. They got him admitted to a boarding school for young boys with the same desire. But after his alcoholic father died, he dropped out of that to support the family as the oldest of seven children.

This also marked the beginning of a "twenty-year temper tantrum against God" over the death of his father. Not long after his father's death, a baby sister died of a brain tumor and his mother killed herself. All the more was he, the eldest child, the major support of his five younger siblings. His temper tantrum meant that he did not attend church, did not pray, and "mostly yelled at God."

In the midst of this alienation from religion, there was, he says, a failed marriage, many affairs, and alcohol abuse. And, "as always happens, an angel in human form was sent to direct him" to AA for treatment for alcohol abuse. This First Step ". . .was the beginning of the Spirit reawakening faith in my soul. I got sober enough to see how destructive my marriage was for both of us and got a divorce." Though sobriety was like a stock market graph, up and down, eventually it became his lifestyle. In timely fashion, "God's grace brought Carol, a cradle-to-grave Presbyterian, into my life." For the first time God was now central in a relationship. Ultimately, the Scripture-based preaching in Carol's church and their relationship to "angel" pastor Rev. Angela and the congregation led to their marriage. Instruction in Reformed theology, the baptism of their son Paul, and membership in the church followed. As he professed that " 'Jesus Christ is my Lord and Savior' all desire for drink left me and took that burden off my shoulders."

Jon's story (part two): Praying to God, "What do you want me to do with the rest of my life?" led to Carol asking Jon if he was thinking of the ministry. His response was "No" the first dozen times. Jon was planning to retire from the public school system after enough financial security to put their son through college and "buy that cabin up north and a fishing boat." It was a good plan, he felt, "but not God's plan." Finally, however, after some time and counseling, he felt that "the Holy Spirit was blowing on the dormant embers of my call to the priesthood." Five years of seminary (evenings and weekends) at Bethel University led to ordination in 2008.

A reflection of mine mentioned my early struggles with preaching. Jon saw these echoed in his own terrors: mumbling, excessive speed, hyperventilating: "The two classes that I took on preaching were some of the worst experiences of my life." Eventually, manuscript preaching (every word printed out) helped him in several venues. Later, scriptural messages about God's mercy and forgiveness struck him: "The Spirit overwhelmed me. I did not open my manuscript. I told my story about God's grace and mercy in my life." So often made flesh in another "angel" along the way.

His self-confidence was reinforced by the impact of this preaching on the congregation so that his theme became: "You are such a sinner, you have been saved by God's grace and mercy through Jesus; therefore you have to preach the Good News." In 2016, he retired from active ministry. "Maybe a cautionary tale, but also a testament to God's grace and mercy."

Tim, a medical doctor, was grieving the death of Jill, his wife of over fifty years. Their relationship clearly had retained a lot of its original freshness. He wrote: "I have been trying to feel the love for Jesus that I felt for Jill. I know the book reasons why I should, but I cannot duplicate that emotional love I had for my wife. I pray for it." A thoughtful look at the commandment in Deuteronomy 6:4-7, later repeated by Jesus, might make any one of us pause: "You shall love the Lord your God with all your heart, and with all your soul, and with all your might."

If we had to feel an emotional love for God such as we feel for a spouse or a dear friend, I think many of us would be in deep trouble. How many of us discuss this over dinner? I did look up Jewish authorities on the commandment as it appears in the Hebrew Bible. They make the point that love for God means desiring to do the will of God, what God asks. To put God's will before all other loyalties. I think it would be rather rare for an ordinary mortal to feel an *emotional* love for God. I'm partial to the idea that we show love for God, apart from emotional feeling, by doing what conscience tells us is the right thing to do, what the teaching of Jesus asks of us regarding our neighbor.

Very likely there may be a mystic or any person who spends several hours a day in prayer who does have ecstatic feelings of love for God. I write, I suppose, as a less fervent believer. Once more, with *feeling*: I think to love God means to do the things God would ask of us: comfort the troubled, take care of the poor, care for suffering or disabled people, be patient with other drivers, gentle with our families and friends.

For some years I have resisted any too facile notion that so-and-so is an angel. (I have no doubt when the reference is to a chubby-cheeked two-year-old. Even after he has smashed a jar of jam on the carpet, he still seems angelic.) My own experience now has me thinking: perhaps I should get over my qualms and join in claiming or re-claiming "angel" for personal belief, for my personal life. Otherwise commerce will take complete control of the term. One reads that originally (outside of Scripture) the term *angel* was used to refer to someone who invested his or her money in the production of a Broadway show. Now in the world of money it is used more broadly. And you or I may feel that the term *angel* is the only, the best way to describe the impact of another person in our life.

The angel may be a stranger or a friend. He or she doesn't have to know that he or she is an angel. Individual beneficiaries of an angel may not be aware of the person's "angelic" status. Does the angel in this case even know what he or she is doing? Personal experience of individuals who show you or me much love or help in some crucial moment convinces us that he or she is an angel. There was another reason for my hesitation: who am I, among the millions of people on this planet, to think that an angel has singled me out? However, of course, a central part of our faith is that God (not a limited being like you and I) loves each of us and that such angels embody that in our lives. Psalm 147:3, 4 tells us that God not only knows the stars by name but heals the brokenhearted. I think some of us, overwhelmed by the goodness of this "angel," feel it's almost "too good to be true." That seems to be the universal response to these human angels. They *make* your day, your week, your month . . . your life.

Notes

1. *Lumen Gentium* (Dogmatic Constitution on the Church) 39, 6, in Austin Flannery, ed., *Vatican Council II: Constitutions, Decrees, Declarations; The Basic Sixteen Documents* (Collegeville, MN: Liturgical Press, 2014).

2. Drew Magary, "The Catholic Church Doesn't Deserve Your Forgiveness," *GQ* (September 12, 2018).

3. Joshua J. McElwee, Heidi Schlumpf, "Exclusive: Cupich says bishops must cede authority, allow lay oversight of accusations," *National Catholic Reporter* (October 15, 2018).

4. Scripture quotations in this book are based on the following: *New Revised Standard Version Bible* © 1989 National Council of the Churches of Christ in the United States of America; *New American Bible, revised edition* © 2010, 1991, 1986, 1970 Confraternity of Christian Doctrine, Washington, D.C.; *The Revised Grail Psalms* © 2010, Conception Abbey/ The Grail, admin. by GIA Publications, Inc.

5. "Pope Francis Releases Letter for Year of Consecrated Life," *Salt and Light Media* (November 29, 2014).

6. Andy Williams, "Yesterday, When I Was Young," lyrics by Charles Aznavour and Fred Ebb (T.R.O. Inc., 1964).

7. Henri J. M. Nouwen, *The Road to Daybreak: A Spiritual Journey* (New York: Doubleday, 1988).

8. David Brooks, "Making Modern Toughness," *The New York Times* (August 30, 2016).

9. Johann Wolfgang von Goethe, "Nur wer die Sehnsucht kennt" (None but the Lonely Heart), in *Wilhelm Meisters Lehrjahre* (Wilhelm Meister's Apprenticeship, 1795).

10. Hank Williams Sr., "I'm So Lonesome I Could Cry" (MGM, 1949).

11. Pope Francis, morning Mass at Casa Santa Marta (December 21, 2017).

12. Video Message of His Holiness Pope Francis to Participants in the 3rd International Symposium on the Apostolic Exhortation *"Amoris Laetitia"* (November 11, 2017).

13. *Catechism of the Catholic Church*, 2nd ed. (United States Catholic Conference—Libreria Editrice Vaticana, 1997), 1776.

14. Almut Furchert, "What to do with Passion Week? Or: Blessed are those who mourn," *Lessons from the Monastery* (blog), cloisterseminars.org (April 16, 2019).

15. Timothy Fry, ed., *The Rule of Saint Benedict 1980* (Collegeville, MN: Liturgical Press, 1981), 7.49, 51.

16. Francis de Sales and Jane de Chantal, *Letters of Spiritual Direction* (New York: Paulist Press, 1988).

17. Brian Wren, "When Christ Was Lifted from the Earth" (Carol Stream, IL: Hope Publishing, 1980).

18. Antonio Spadaro, "A Big Heart Open to God: An interview with Pope Francis," *America* (September 30, 2013).

19. Terry Gross, "This Pig Wants to Party: Maurice Sendak's Latest," *Fresh Air* (September 20, 2011).

20. Spadaro, "A Big Heart Open to God."

21. Seneca, *Moral Letters to Lucilius*, Letter 28.

22. Barbara Kingsolver, "Quality Time," in *Homeland and Other Stories* (New York: Harper Perennial, 1990).

23. Shakespeare, *The Tempest*, act V, scene 1.

24. Message of His Holiness Pope Francis for the World Day of Migrants and Refugees (January 17, 2016).

25. Message of His Holiness Pope Francis on the twenty-fifth anniversary of the fall of the Berlin Wall (November 9, 2014).

26. Message of His Holiness Pope Francis, homily for the Ordinary Public Consistory for the Creation of New Cardinals (November 19, 2016).

27. Message of His Holiness Pope Francis, "God of Surprises," morning meditation in the Chapel of the Domus Sanctae Marthae (May 8, 2017).

28. G. K. Chesterton, "Evening," in *Volume 10: Collected Poetry, Part I* (San Francisco: Ignatius Press, 1994).

29. Irving Berlin, "I Got the Sun in the Mornin'" from *Annie Get Your Gun* (1946).

30. Henri J. M. Nouwen, *Our Greatest Gift: A Meditation on Dying and Caring* (San Francisco: HarperOne, 1994), 17.

31. Cardinal Léon Joseph Suenens, *A New Pentecost?* (San Francisco: HarperOne, 1974).

32. Coventry Patmore, "The Toys," in *The Oxford Book of English Verse: 1250–1918*, ed. Arthur Quiller-Couch (Oxford, UK: Oxford University Press, 1963).

33. Ralph Waldo Emerson, "The World-Soul," *Poems* (New York: Houghton, Mifflin, 1904).

34. Excerpt from the English translation of *The Roman Missal* © 2010, International Commission on English in the Liturgy Corporation. All rights reserved.

35. Henri J. M. Nouwen, *With Burning Hearts: A Meditation on the Eucharistic Life* (Maryknoll, NY: Orbis Books, 2003).

36. First Message of His Holiness Benedict XVI at the End of the Eucharistic Concelebration with the Members of the College of Cardinals in the Sistine Chapel (April 20, 2005).

37. John Henry Newman, "The Pillar of the Cloud," in *A Victorian Anthology, 1837–1895*, ed. Edmund Clarence Stedman (Cambridge, MA: Riverside Press, 1895).

38. Quoted in Nancy Mairs, *A Dynamic God: Living an Unconventional Catholic Faith* (Boston, MA: Beacon Press, 2007).

39. Aldous Huxley, "The Rest Is Silence," in *Music at Night and Other Essays* (Garden City, NY: Doubleday, Doran, 1931).

40. Pope Francis, "The Future You," TED talk, Vancouver, BC (April 25, 2017).

41. Martha White, ed., *In the Words of E. B. White: Quotations from America's Most Companionable of Writers* (Ithaca, NY: Cornell University Press, 2011).

42. Rosemary Lloyd, *Baudelaire's World* (Ithaca, NY: Cornell University Press, 2002).

43. Quoted in George Vass, *A Pattern of Doctrines 2: The Atonement and Mankind's Salvation, Understanding Karl Rahner, Volume 4* (London: Sheed & Ward, 1998).

44. Henry Hitchings, *Sorry!: The English and Their Manners* (New York: Farrar, Straus and Giroux, 2013).

45. Louis Armstrong, "What a Wonderful World," lyrics by Bob Thiele (ABC, 1967).

46. W. H. Auden, in the introduction to *Italian Journey* by Goethe (London, 1962).

47. Miguel de Unamuno, *The Tragic Sense of Life in Men and in Peoples* (London: MacMillan, 1926).

48. *Calvin and Hobbes*, Minneapolis *Star Tribune* (April 5, 1995).

49. Abraham Joshua Heschel, *Between God and Man: An Interpretation of Judaism from the Writings of Abraham Joshua Heschel*, ed. Fritz A. Rothschild (New York: Simon & Schuster, 1959).

50. Lao-Tzu, *Tao Te Ching*, trans. Stephen Addiss and Stanley Lombardo (Boston, MA: Shambhala, 2007).

51. Huxley, "The Rest is Silence."

52. Elizabeth Wurtzel, *Prozac Nation: Young and Depressed in America* (New York: Riverhead Books, 1994).

53. Pope Paul VI, *Nostra Aetate* (Declaration on the Relation of the Church to Non-Christian Religions, October 28, 1965) 2.

54. Pope Francis, *Evangelii Gaudium* (The Joy of the Gospel, November 24, 2013) 114.

55. Reinhold Niebuhr, *The Irony of American History* (Chicago: University of Chicago Press, 2008).

56. H. L. Mencken, *A Second Mencken Chrestomathy: A New Selection from the Writings of America's Legendary Editor, Critic, and Wit* (Baltimore: The Johns Hopkins University Press, 2006).

57. Robert Southwell, "Times Go by Turns," in *The Oxford Book of English Verse: 1250–1918*.

58. Jeffrey Kluger, "The Cathedral of Science: The elusive Higgs boson is at last found—and the Universe gets a little less mysterious," *Time Magazine* (July 23, 2012).

59. Pope Francis, *Amoris Laetitia* (The Joy of Love, March 19, 2016) 304.

60. Pope Francis, *God Is Always Near: Conversations with Pope Francis*, ed. Gary Seromik (Huntington, IN: Our Sunday Visitor, 2015).

61. Roberta Bondi, *Memories of God: Theological Reflections on a Life* (Nashville: Abingdon Press, 1995).

62. Eric Milner-White and George Wallace Brigg, *Daily Prayer* (London: Oxford, 1941).

63. Mark Kemp, "Q&A: Jimmy Buffett," *Rolling Stone* (August 22, 1996).

64. Jan Michael Joncas, "On Eagle's Wings" (Portland, OR: OCP Publications, 1979).

65. Pope Francis, *Evangelii Gaudium* 43.

66. Diana L. Eck, *Encountering God: A Spiritual Journey from Bozeman to Banaras* (Boston, MA: Beacon Press, 2014).

67. Simon-Joseph Pellegrin, "O Come, Divine Messiah," trans. Sr. Mary of St. Philip (1877).

68. Margaret Visser, *The Gift of Thanks: The Roots and Rituals of Gratitude* (Boston, MA: Houghton Mifflin Harcourt, 2009).